RIDING ON High Hills

TRAINING THE CHURCH IN LOVE

ALISON VEAZEY, KERRY L SKINNER
with JOSH SAEFKOW

Graphic Designer: Cover design by:
Jay Adcock, jay@adcockcreativegroup.com

Cover Photo: Randy Fitzgerald

Riding on High Hills
Training the Church in Love
Isaiah 58:13-14

Alison Veazey   Kerry L. Skinner   Josh Saefkow

Riding on High Hills
Copyright © 2024 by Alison Veazey and Kerry L. Skinner
Think LifeChange Institute of Biblical Counseling
www.thinklifechange.com

Library of Congress Cataloging-in-Publication Data

Skinner, Kerry L., 1955–
    My Spirit is Life and Peace/Alison Veazey/Kerry L. Skinner, 1st edition
    p. cm.
    Includes bibliographic references.

    ISBN 978-1-931080-28-6

1. Personal Growth–Religious aspects–Christianity
2. Counseling–Biblical teaching

All rights reserved. Printed in the United States of America. No part of this book may be used or reproduced in any manner whatsoever without written permission except in the case of brief quotations embodied in critical articles and reviews. For more information address:

www.thinklifechange.com

Unless otherwise indicated, all Scripture quotations are taken from *The Holy Bible, New King James Version.* © 1982 by Thomas Nelson, Inc. Used by permission of Thomas Nelson, Inc.

Contents

Section One: The Heart's Posture 9

Chapter 1–A Solid Foundation 10

Chapter 2–Making the Adjustment 26

Chapter 3–Finding Rest in the Release 46

Section Two: The Church's Posture 63

Chapter 4–Honor through Submission 64

Chapter 5–Surrendering Your Way 92

Chapter 6–Joy in the Body 110

Section Three: The Lord's Blessing 131

Chapter 7–Honor from God 132

Chapter 8–Living in God's Promise 150

Chapter 9–Confidence in God 168

Appendix: Other Works 185

Dedication

To God our Savior, Who alone is wise, Be glory and majesty, Dominion and power, Both now and forever. Amen.
Jude 25

Introduction

I was broken, stressed, confused, and angry. The burden of a grudge affected my attitude and actions–have you ever been there? My prayers sounded like the old Irish prayer, "Lord, as for my enemies, please turn their hearts. If not, please turn their ankles so I will know them by their limp." Everywhere I looked, it seemed as if everyone had twisted ankles. It is not a good look when you, as a pastor, are praying for people to have broken ankles so you can recognize them as an enemy. I quickly was learning I cannot have a church representing the Lord Jesus Christ if I am not in a right relationship with Him. God was revealing things in my heart such as the desire to please people and the need for approval. My sin was hindering my relationship with God and others. I needed to change.

Two dear friends, Alison Veazey and Kerry Skinner, came into my life. Kerry gently but confidently spoke into my life about God's desire for me to have a healthy relationship with Himself, but my pride stood in the way, and I needed to repent.

The Holy Spirit of God met me with kindness as I called out to Jesus for forgiveness and cleansing. I experienced what Jesus promised in Matthew 11:28-30, "Come to Me, all you who labor and are heavy laden, and I will give you rest. Take My yoke upon you and learn from Me, for I am gentle and lowly in heart, and you will find rest for your souls. For My yoke is easy and My burden is light."

The book you hold in your hand has the power to release you from life's hurts and hang-ups. You, too, can find rest for your wearied soul. I recently visited with my friend, Pastor Benny Tate, of *Rock Springs Church* in Milner, Georgia. I was expressing my desire to finish well. He stopped me and said, "Josh, many are finishing well, but they are not well when they finish."

This book allows you to be well in all seasons of life. The Scripture and parables within this work will guide you through life's difficulties. I pray you find the healing I have experienced through the joy of repentance and enjoy God's Presence while riding on high hills.

Pastor Josh Saefkow
Flat Creek Baptist Church
Fayetteville, Georgia

Section One:

The Heart's Posture

Riding on High Hills

Chapter 1: A Solid Foundation

RIDING PRINCIPLE # 1

BODY POSITION: HEELS DOWN

Horseback riding is grounded in balance. The best riders balance their bodies in such a way that it appears they are doing absolutely nothing, but that is not the case. A lot of work goes into training the position of the body for solid, safe, and balanced riding. For some this balance comes more natural, but for others it requires much training. When you are sitting on top of a large animal there are circumstances that are out of your control, but a balanced rider can handle difficult circumstances. It is true that you can hold on and brace when a challenge arises, but confidence comes through stability and stability through consistency. There are three major positions that we will focus on for the next three chapters. The first one is the position of your feet.

A major principle in horseback riding is that you must keep your heels down. When your heels are down and you are in proper position, you are secure and stable. You are ready for sudden movements from the horse whether that involves the horse spooking at an object, jumping over a jump, or moving suddenly. Keeping your heels down is an anchor for your weight, but it is not natural. It requires conditioning your muscles to stay in that position. When someone begins to learn to ride a horse the most common position of the feet would be toes down. This is the most unstable place for your feet. The reason is because it makes your upper body lean forward. When your upper body leans forward, any sudden movement may push your body further forward and ultimately result in a fall. You do not want to get ahead of the horse or fall behind the horse with your body. Therefore, the most balanced place is in the center of the horse's movement.

> Confidence comes through stability and stability through consistency.

The first step to success in this position is to make sure that your stirrups are the right length. This means using your equipment properly. The way to find the proper length of the stirrup is to sit on the back of the horse with your legs hanging down. The proper length is when the bottom of the stirrup rests at your ankle. Then place your foot in the stirrup and place all of your weight into your heels with your heels down and toes up. Initially this is not a comfortable position, but as your muscles stretch, your feet will begin to stay in that position without having to constantly think about it. Your muscles have memory. As you practice, muscle memory will begin to kick in. This allows the mind to focus on other aspects of riding.

Any foundation takes time to develop. To have a solid foundation in riding you must come to the place where your body balances without thought. This is the safest position to be in when any obstacle arises. But many only want to have fun and enjoy the ride. Therefore, most do not take the time to build a solid foundation. This results in instability. While you may be able to get away with it for a while, there will come a time when you will fall. Take the time to train your body to keep your heels down.

Chapter 1
A Solid Foundation

"...If you turn away your foot from the Sabbath..."
Isaiah 58:13

In 2015, God called Alison's family out of a mega church to a much smaller church in Texas where Kerry Skinner was the pastor. For the next three years, Kerry discipled Alison, and she grew closer to Christ. During that time God laid it on their hearts to start *Think LifeChange Institute of Biblical Counseling*. Alison also started a ministry called *Victory Reins* which uses horses in Biblical counseling. Little did Kerry and Alison know that nearly 800 miles away in the state of Georgia a horse-loving pastor was following *Victory Reins*.

In 2017, when Kerry and Alison began *Think LifeChange*, Kerry decided to step down from his role as senior pastor. In doing so he and his wife Elaine forfeited his salary and were unable to stay in Texas due to the cost of living. They previously lived in Georgia in the 1990s. Kerry and Elaine returned to that area to develop *Think LifeChange*. They had no idea at the time that the horse-loving pastor who was following *Victory Reins* lived only thirty minutes away.

One of the roles of *Think LifeChange* was to visit area churches in order to inform pastors of their ministry. One of those churches was *Flat Creek Baptist Church* in Fayetteville, Georgia. Do you have any idea who the pastor was? The pastor of Flat Creek Baptist Church you may have guessed was Josh Sacfkow, the horse-loving pastor. Pastor Josh met with Kerry on October 19, 2021. Kerry shared about *Victory*

Reins, and Josh explained that he had been following the ministry online. Kerry did not believe Josh because there had been little activity on the website at that time. Kerry thought Josh might be thinking of another ministry. But as they continued talking, it became clear that pastor Josh was in fact following the *Victory Reins* website[1]. From that point on the relationship between *Flat Creek Baptist Church* and *Think LifeChange/Victory Reins* began to develop. Only God could have made this connection.

In April 2022, *Victory Reins* held a certification training. Alison invited Josh to attend. A few months after the certification training, *Victory Reins* held a demonstration where Josh shared his testimony regarding his initial experience at the training. Here is his testimony:

> *This past year has been pretty difficult. The church has had above average growth, and while that sounds awesome, it definitely brings challenges. I started receiving letters from people who were literally picking apart my life. It seemed as though they attended church only to find the flaws that I was most insecure about. These letters really messed with my mind. In fact, I was getting to a place where I was so stressed out that I thought something was wrong with my brain. I told my wife Kelsie, who is a nurse, that I needed to go to the doctor because I thought I had cancer. She was concerned as well but did not think I had cancer. Her concern was that I wasn't sleeping and the stress was piling on.*
>
> *On the morning that I was heading out to attend the Victory Reins certification training, I went to the church to unlock the doors for a new hire. When I arrived, I realized that I forgot my keys. I began to cry. I was so mad because I had one job to do and I blew it. My two daughters also knew that I was stressed. This incident was a reflection of how I felt. I wanted to win for my family and the church. I wanted everyone to know that I cared about them and that I loved them. Even though we have a healthy, growing church, it is so important to me that they know that I love them. I felt like I was failing miserably.*

---

1 Victory Reins can now be found at https://thinklifechange.com/victory-reins/.

This all went down right before I arrived for the Victory Reins training. The first activity of the program was to groom a horse. One thing that you should know about me is that I like efficiency. I work quickly. Therefore, approaching this task was no different. We had fifteen minutes to spend with the horse without talking. Fifteen minutes with no talking to an extrovert is torture. As we began the activity, I took all the brushes and put them in my pockets and started grooming. It took me five minutes to groom, and then I just stood there leaning on the horse. I noticed that the leaders were taking notes.

I started looking around and saw the other guys were still grooming. I realized that I missed the lesson. I was not doing this well. Sure enough they pointed it out quickly. They noticed that I was the only one who had all the brushes in his pockets. I recognized that for me it was about completing the task and moving on to the next thing. However, the activity was centered around building a relationship with the horse, not completing the task.

My mind was always on the next crisis situation. I was not focused on building my relationship with God. Instead I was focused on doing His business, and that was causing a lot of stress. I was trying to lead people in my own power to places that they did not want to be led. I had so much anxiety. The truth was presented and it really confronted the real issue of my heart. I realized I loved people more than I loved God. This was all revealed through a grooming exercise.

When Alison shared that we are to love God first and then people, she was one hundred percent correct. I needed to go back to my first love, the Lord. My next question was regarding what the process of repentance looks like. Keep in mind that I have degrees in higher education but now I was asking a simple question: What does the process of repentance look like for a follower of Jesus? I thought repentance was for an unbeliever to become a believer.

> I loved people more than I loved God... I needed to go back to my first love, the Lord.

> *Another thing that added to my anxiety was that when I went to a committee meeting and told them that I was feeling pressure, they looked me right in the eye and said, 'Everybody can get discouraged in this church but you. This is a season that we need you to be strong.' I get what they were trying to say, but the truth was that through this process, God humbled me and I realized that I couldn't carry that. I must return to my first love.*

Pastor Josh is not the only believer who has at times reversed the first and second commandment taught by Jesus. The proper order found in Scripture states, "'You shall love the Lord your God with all your heart, with all your soul, and with all your mind.' This is the first and great commandment. And the second is like it: "You shall love your neighbor as yourself'" (Matthew 22:37-39). In the pursuit to obey these commands, there is a tendency to reverse them and put people before God. You cannot substitute loving people for building a relationship with God. When you do you begin to feel as though you are being pulled in many directions. The reason for this feeling is that you cannot do Kingdom work without the King. When you are loving God with all your heart, then you will be at peace. This brings rest not anxiety. Therefore, if you recognize anxiety in your heart, then you may have left your first love.

> You cannot substitute loving people for building a relationship with God.

God used horses, the church, and the message of repentance to connect Kerry, Alison, and Josh. Because of that this book is unique in that it will combine the principles of horseback riding with God's command regarding the Sabbath with the intent to train the church in love.

The Sabbath

> *"...If you turn away your foot from the Sabbath..."*
> **Isaiah 58:13**

While praying to write this book, God directed Alison to two verses of Scripture that encompass God's desire for His people to return to Him. In order to truly unpack the depth of these verses, they will be presented one at a time in each chapter of the book. To begin it is critical that you understand that words matter, especially the words of God. As the Holy Spirit guides you through this book it is important to return to God's desire regarding the Sabbath. This may require an acceptance that you have drifted from the true intention of this day of rest. Hopefully this will grant you an understanding of why God is so adamant about the Sabbath and how it directly relates to the condition of your heart.

The Sabbath day was provided by God as a day of rest. But the religious leaders took this day created for people by God and turned it into their own way to control people. The Sabbath is simply a day of rest. "Then God blessed the seventh day and sanctified it, because in it He rested from all His work which God had created and made." (Genesis 2:3). In sanctifying the seventh day, God made it holy. He set it apart for sacred use.

From the time of creation to the time of Isaiah, people completely drifted from God's blessing of the Sabbath. From the outside, it seemed as though they continued to honor the Sabbath but this was in ritual only. God saw the condition of their hearts. The Sabbath can be mistaken as attending church, tithing, and performing outward offerings. While all of these are included in this day, God's intention for the Sabbath is rest for the heart. A heart of love toward God produces outward offerings, but outward offerings alone do not produce rest in the heart.

The people of God in Isaiah's day failed miserably in giving themselves to God. They started out right but ultimately drifted from the Heart of God. They attempted to perform everything in worship as per the law, but they missed the point because their heart was far from God. As a believer, you cannot be at rest when your heart is not in right relationship with the Lord. God's people were more concerned with physical rest on the Sabbath than having their heart at rest with God. It is clear that not much has changed regarding the Sabbath in the church today.

> A heart of love toward God produces outward offerings, but outward offerings alone do not produce rest in the heart.

Kerry was leading a conference in a church several years ago on *The Heart of the Problem*, a book that he co-authored with Dr. Henry Brandt. Here is his testimony regarding that conference:

> *The pastor invited me to lead the conference and preach on Sunday morning. I accepted his invitation. The church was not a Baptist church so they did things differently than I was used to. I observed the activity during the time of worship. The people in this church were wild in comparison to what I had previously experienced. They were swaying and shouting, "Praise the Lord!" It was a very exciting time.*
>
> *Then the pastor introduced me and asked me to come and preach. I shared a few thoughts like this:*
>
> *"Your husband or wife do not make you like you are, they reveal what you are."*
>
> *"Other people cannot put sin within you."*
>
> *"What comes out of your mouth proceeds from your heart."*
>
> *As I was speaking, I noticed that the same people who were excited during worship, were now getting quieter and quieter. Nobody was saying, "Amen." No one was shouting, "Hallelujah."*
>
> *My dad was there with me, and afterwards he said, "Kerry, couldn't you have just preached on heaven so we could say amen." Instead, I talked about the process of sin and how there is no human remedy.*
>
> *When I was finished preaching, I gave the invitation and nearly everyone who was in the choir came to the altar. God did an amazing work. People began to weep as they were praying. Some of them were sobbing out loud. Then the weeping started to spread through the worship center. People were sobbing, saying, "Oh, God, look at my heart. I am not where I need to be." It was an awesome time.*
>
> *When the invitation was over, the pastor looked at me and said, "Kerry, could you come and help us process what God just did?" I said, "Pastor, are you sure you want me to do that?" He said, "I really do." I said to the people. "I don't understand." When I came in you were having praise and worship and you were very excited and were lifting your*

hands. You were clapping and saying, "Amen and Hallelujah." But now the ones that were leading worship are the ones who are down here repenting of sin. What was happening in the service before the invitation? You cannot worship God with a dirty heart. The pastor and congregation were convinced that much of the prior, "so called worship" was not true worship from the heart.

What happened during that service is the same thing that was happening in the first chapter of Isaiah. The people were praising God with their lips, with what appeared as outward obedience, but their hearts were far from Him. Praise is not acceptable to God if the one who is praising God is not acceptable to God. Therefore, the Sabbath is much more than going to church on Sunday, singing songs, and then going home.

The religious leaders in Jesus' day took God's command to honor the Sabbath and added so many man-made rules to it that it was nearly impossible to follow. They took a day of rest and made it burdensome. They even tried to catch Jesus and His disciples breaking the Sabbath. Jesus and His disciples plucked the heads of grain in the field to eat on the Sabbath day, and the Pharisees asked Jesus: "Look, why do they do what is not lawful on the Sabbath?" (Mark 2:23-24).

> **Praise is not acceptable to God if the one who is praising God is not acceptable to God.**

And He said to them, "The Sabbath was made for man, and not man for the Sabbath. Therefore the Son of Man is also Lord of the Sabbath."

Mark 2:27-28

The Pharisees were not interested in having Jesus and His disciples follow the law. They were interested in catching them in an act of disobeying the system that they created. They were always trying to trap Jesus because His teaching threatened their man-made system. The Pharisees had taken God's commandment to keep the Sabbath holy and added so many rules to it that it did not provide rest, but bondage.

Jesus responded to them by reminding them of the time that David ran from Saul and stopped to get food from the high priest. The high priest gave David the showbread, which was not lawful to eat except for the priests. The high priest did not break the law, because he provided for David (See 1 Samuel 21:1-6). When we become focused on following the law, we lose sight of the Spirit. Loving someone in need is walking in the Spirit of Christ. When the Pharisees' tried to trap Jesus and His disciples, they revealed that their hearts were far from God. They were not interested in love, they were interested in staying in control. Can you imagine telling the Lord of the Sabbath what He should do on the Sabbath? As a believer we are to look to Jesus to guide us through His Spirit. If Jesus allowed His disciples to eat the grain on the Sabbath, then how can man tell him that it is unlawful?

The response from Jesus that the Sabbath was made for man and not man for the Sabbath reveals that the Spirit of the Sabbath is love for man. It was never intended to put people in bondage, but rather to provide them with rest. When the Lord commanded the Israelites to turn their foot from the Sabbath, He meant that they were trampling on His design for the Sabbath. The people in Isaiah's day, in Jesus' day, and in our day were and still are trampling on the Sabbath by not surrendering their hearts to the Lord. What type of heart would trample on the Sabbath?

The Heart's Posture

The spiritual heart is the seat of a person's will, emotions, and thoughts. In order to have a solid spiritual foundation, the heart must be surrendered to Jesus. The people of God in Isaiah's day had rebellious hearts that were trampling on God's design. The Pharisee's in Jesus' day had hard hearts and were only concerned in following the system that they created, not in helping the people obey God. People today have the same problem. The spiritual heart has not changed since the fall of man in the garden. Time, culture, or background does not indicate the state of a person's spiritual heart. According to Scripture there are many different foundations of a person's spiritual heart. The heart not surrendered to God can be hard (see Exodus 4:21), stiff (see Acts

7:51), deceived (see Deuteronomy 11:16), confused (see Deuteronomy 28:28), proud, or rebellious. The heart surrendered to God is willing (see Exodus 25:2), glad (see Deuteronomy 28:47), wise and understanding (see 1 Kings 3:12), has integrity (1 Kings 9:4), is obedient (see Romans 6:17), and is pure and honest. As long as the heart's posture leans toward the world and is not surrendered to the Lord, there is no solid foundation in Christ.

Scripture has much to say about the heart of a person. In order to turn away your foot from the Sabbath, as God commanded, you must examine the condition of your heart. While outward change and obedience may fool other people, it will not fool God. It is only a matter of time before you will fall. What type of heart would trample on the Sabbath? A heart that is not surrendered to Jesus. Therefore, the foundation of your heart is centered on your love and faith in Jesus. There is no other way. Until your heart is surrendered to the Holy Spirit, you will not have a solid foundation.

Pastor Josh was struggling when he arrived at *Victory Reins*. God showed him the condition of his heart in order to set him free. Josh was sensitive to the Holy Spirit and was able to recognize what the Spirit was revealing to him. He repented and was restored in his love relationship with Jesus. But that does not mean that his heart will never struggle again. The point is that when one does struggle again, you must take it to God in repentance in order to restore fellowship with Him. Many have come face to face to a besetting sin in their life and have not turned to God in repentance. Those who respond this way will be tossed around with every struggle in their life.

In order for the heart to stay in the right posture toward God, it must be trained by the Holy Spirit in love. This means hearing from the Lord through His Word, repenting of any known sin, and making the adjustment. If you have been trampling on the Sabbath and are ready to turn to the Lord you can do that today.

Put your heels down and join us as we learn to *Ride on High Hills*.

Riding on High Hills

Riding on High Hills Devotion Chapter 1

A Solid Foundation

"...If you turn away your foot from the Sabbath..."
Isaiah 58:13

Much like horseback riding, staying grounded in Christ requires balance. Consider your feet for a moment and what they are designed to accomplish for your body. Your feet allow you to walk with balance. However, they can also be used to stomp or trample on things. This is what God is describing in this verse of Scripture. The Israelites had completely left the ways of God and were following their own ways. It is interesting that out of all the ten commandments, God chose the commandment to "keep the Sabbath Holy" as the condition for them to turn back to Him. This is because they were dishonoring what He created for them by continuing in religious (church) activity with a heart that was far from Him. The command had no value to them as long as their hearts were not in it. There is no balance or strength in your spiritual life if your heart is far from Jesus, even if you do all the "church activity."

God designed the Sabbath for rest. If there is one thing people are lacking in church today it is rest. More than physical rest, the Sabbath is rest for the heart, soul, and mind. While refraining from labor is part of the Sabbath, it is much more than that: it is a heart surrendered to Christ. Think back to the position of the foot in horseback riding and consider that when your heel is down, you cannot stomp on anything. This is a picture of turning away your foot from the Sabbath. To embrace what the Lord designed for you keeps great balance in your spiritual life. When your heart is at rest in Christ, the weight of your soul is in His Hands. Jesus is your anchor to confidence and security. A believer who is balanced in his relationship with Jesus can handle difficult circumstances and not fall at every trial or temptation.

After the fall to sin in the garden, God gave a curse to the woman, man, and the serpent. The Scripture states, "And I will put enmity between you [the serpent] and the woman, and between your seed and her Seed; he shall bruise your head, and you shall bruise His heel." (Genesis 3:15). This is enmity between Jesus and Satan. Jesus has power over Satan, but when Jesus came to earth He was in human form. Satan's temptation on Jesus in Matthew 4:1-11 was completely focused on his weak human nature, His heel. This means that Satan's temptation on you, as a follower of Jesus, will be on your human nature. The difference between you and Jesus is that you have a sinful nature. When you allow your sinful nature to control your life, it is like riding a horse with your toes pointed down. There is no balance or security in that position. While Satan may still come after you with your heels down, he will be unable to cause you to fall due to the fact that your heart is set on the only power that defeated him, the power of Jesus.

Heart's Posture #1
Learn to put your heels down by surrendering your heart to Christ. It is the first step in delighting in the Lord and riding on high hills.

The Rider's Position #1
Always keep your heels down.

Chapter 1: A Solid Foundation

Riding on High Hills

Riding Principle #2

Body Position: Eyes Up

Another important part of your body for horseback riding is your eyes. Most riders struggle because they tend to look down at the horse or the ground instead of where they want to go. Looking down takes your body out of balance. Let's take a moment to demonstrate how much the body moves with the look of the eye. Sit up and look straight ahead. Then, turn your eye to the left of your body and look at the ground. When you do, pay attention to what happens to your upper and lower body. You should notice that when you move your eyes to this position it moves your upper body and also your hips.

Horses are in tune with your body movement. As you move your body you are communicating with them. When your body is out of balance, it is hard for them to adjust. Horseback riding takes many adjustments because there are many variables. You must train your body to be in the proper position. The body follows the eyes. When you turn your head to look to the right or the left your upper body moves with it. To stay balanced you must look up at where you are going. A common mistake is to look at what you are trying to avoid. For example, if there is a tree that you want to avoid the common tendency is to look at the tree. This tends to lead the horse to the tree. Instead, set your eyes on where you want to go instead of what you want to avoid. When you do that you will avoid potential danger.

> Horseback riding takes many adjustments because there are many variables.

Riding on High Hills

Chapter 2
Making the Adjustment

"... From doing your pleasure on My Holy day..."
Isaiah 58:13

When this book project began, pastor Josh was beginning a sermon series on the book of Jude. After listening to his first sermon on this book of the Bible, it became evident that these sermons would be a main focus in this book. Jude starts the letter with providing a caution to those in the church. Considering the state of our churches today, it only seems fitting to share the truths from these verses. While it would seem better to focus on what makes you feel good, feeling good will not change the state of your heart nor consequently the state of the church. God's response to the church is a direct reflection of the state of the church. The church sometimes needs rebuke and correction and therefore, God led this book in that direction.

It would seem that even Jude faced this dilemma in what he was writing to the church. Pastor Josh speaks of it in his sermon. Jude writes: "Beloved, while I was very diligent to write to you concerning our common salvation, I found it necessary to write to you exhorting you to contend earnestly for the faith which was once for all delivered to the saints" (Jude 3). Pastor Josh states, "While Jude wanted to write in a way that was going to explain salvation, he instead presses pause. Impressed by the Holy Spirit he states that it was necessary for him to write to you that you would fight and contend for the faith." This is fitting for our churches today because many pastors continuously preach on salvation without addressing the fact that there are "certain men that have crept in unnoticed" (Jude 4). There are some who have come into the church through stealth. If leaders only preach salvation to the lost, they neglect dealing with those set on destroying the church.

Additionally, leaders will not move with the Spirit if they have a personal agenda. This happened in Isaiah's day. God wanted the people to refrain, "from doing your [their] pleasure on My [His] Holy day" (Isaiah 58:13). This verse may bring to mind those who do not attend church and instead have fun on Sundays. However, this verse also applies to leaders leading church services according to what pleases themselves.

In order to make an adjustment the people of God must open their spiritual eyes to see what is really happening. Godless people are attempting to destroy God's leadership. They will try to discredit, lie, and manufacture false stories in order to short circuit the activity of God. Those who rebel against the Lord cannot give correct instruction. Although they may deceive others into thinking they are Christians, they are not accomplishing righteousness.

> Godless people are attempting to destroy God's leadership.

These people are ungodly. They turn God's beautiful and marvelous grace into a completely false concept. They use it as a license to sin. They convince themselves that they can engage in immoral activity and receive approval because of grace. This is a complete lie. Anything provided to you by God is designed to make you more like Jesus. Therefore, to believe that God's grace would go against His nature is far from the Truth.

While it is true that our society's cultural laws change, God's moral law never changes. It will always be wrong to steal, kill, lie, covet, and commit adultery. It will always be wrong to trample on the Sabbath. The fourth commandment states, "Remember the Sabbath day, to keep it holy" (Exodus 20:8).

> It will always be wrong to steal, kill, lie, covet, and commit adultery.

Chapter 2: Making the Adjustment

Six days you shall labor and do all your work, but the seventh day is the Sabbath of the LORD your God. In it you shall do no work: you, nor your son, nor your daughter, nor your male servant, nor your female servant, nor your cattle, nor your stranger who is within your gates. For in six days the LORD made the heavens and the earth, the sea, and all that is in them, and rested the seventh day. Therefore the LORD blessed the Sabbath day and hallowed it.

Exodus 20:9-11

The commandments are not a list of rules dictated by a mean God. Rather, they are boundary lines issued by a loving God to protect His people. When you approach the Sabbath day as a command from a mean God, you completely miss the Spirit of the command. Every command provided by God is based on a Spirit of Love. God has your best interest at heart. He does not command you to keep the Sabbath day Holy as a punishment, but He commands the Sabbath in order to deepen your relationship with Him. His desire is to protect your heart in such a way that you remain in fellowship with Him. When you continuously do your pleasure on His Holy day, He will not remain in fellowship with you because He will not fellowship with sin.

> The commandments are boundary lines issued by a loving God to protect His people... Every command provided by God is based upon a Spirit of Love. God has your best interest at heart.

My Holy Day

To fully grasp the fourth commandment, it is important to understand the three commandments that precede it. The first four commandments portray your relationship with God. Keep in mind that God will not fellowship with sin, therefore, if you are guilty of breaking the first three commandments, then you will not "stop doing your pleasure" on the Lord's Holy day. The only way to honor Him is to commit your heart to Him. Anything less than that is not acceptable to the Lord.

Let's take a look at the first three commandments in order to gain an understanding of keeping our hearts right before a Holy God:

You shall have no other gods before Me.
Exodus 20:3

You shall not make for yourself a carved image—any likeness of anything that is in heaven above, or that is in the earth beneath, or that is in the water under the earth; you shall not bow down to them nor serve them. For I, the LORD your God, am a jealous God, visiting the iniquity of the fathers upon the children to the third and fourth generations of those who hate Me, but showing mercy to thousands, to those who love Me and keep My commandments.
Exodus 20:4-6

You shall not take the name of the LORD your God in vain, for the LORD will not hold him guiltless who takes His name in vain.
Exodus 20:7

Without a grasp on the first three commandments, you will not fully understand why God addresses keeping the Sabbath Holy. When you are obedient to the first three, you are in a right relationship with God and desire to keep His day holy. God's command in Isaiah 58:13 addressed the Israelites' hearts. They were keeping the desires of their own hearts and worshipping idols. God addressed this because of His Love for them. As long as they were in rebellion, God could not help them grow because He will not be in fellowship with sin. The ten commandments are designed to reveal sin and lead one to the Love of God.

> The ten commandments are designed to reveal sin and lead one to the Love of God.

The Condition of the Heart

God is the only One who understands the condition of the heart. This is why He commanded Adam and Eve to avoid the tree of good and evil (See Genesis 2:16-17). He knew if they ate of this tree their hearts would turn away from Him. In the book of Jude, there are three examples of those who have turned away from the Lord. "Woe to them! For they have gone in the way of Cain, have run greedily in the error of Balaam for profit, and perished in the rebellion of Korah" (Jude 11).

Chapter 2: Making the Adjustment

The first reference that Jude warns the church about is "the way of Cain." This story is found in Genesis 4:1-15. Cain and his brother Abel brought a sacrifice to the Lord and the Lord accepted Abel's sacrifice but did not accept Cain's. Pastor Josh addressed this in his sermon stating, "God did not accept Cain's offering because of the condition of Cain's heart." God also addressed this in the book of Isaiah:

> *Therefore the Lord said: "Inasmuch as these people draw near with their mouths and honor Me with their lips, but have removed their hearts far from Me, and their fear toward Me is taught by the commandment of men,*
>
> **Isaiah 29:13**

Pastor Josh described Cain's condition,

> *Cain was that person. He tried to honor the Lord with his offering, but it was not acceptable because his heart was far from Him. The conflict that Cain had with God was in his heart, not in his offering. God is not interested in your offering if your heart is not in it. Cain rejected God's Way and chose his own way. Apostates will always tamper with salvation. They will move in and try to work in some kind of man-made religion. Yet, the only way to salvation is to surrender to God through Jesus Christ Who is holy.*

> **The conflict that Cain had with God was in his heart, not in his offering.**

Cain is the first murderer in the Bible. Even though God tried to protect Cain, Cain ignored God and went his own way. When you disregard your relationship with God by breaking the first four commandments, you are open to breaking the rest of the commandments that represent your relationship with people.

Cain not only rejected God, but he also turned toward the way of the devil.

> *...not as Cain who was of the wicked one and murdered his brother. And why did he murder him? Because his works were evil and his brother's righteous.*
>
> **1 John 3:12**

These men in Jude's day did not practice selfless ways but their own ways. Their hearts lead them away from the Ways of God. They worshipped themselves rather than their Creator. Their major sin was breaking fellowship with God by breaking the commands that would have kept them in His Love. Just because you tithe at church does not mean your gift is acceptable to the Lord. You must check the condition of your heart. God is not interested in the act of giving as much as He is interested in a giving heart surrendered to His Way. The conflict lies in the condition of your heart. Cain's way was to get rid of his brother; God's Way was to change Cain's heart. Many in churches today claim to worship the Lord even though hearts are far from Him. God is interested in changing your heart that you may go His Way and not your own.

> They worshipped themselves rather than their Creator.

The second warning Jude gives is the error of Balaam. Pastor Josh taught that, "Balaam was a prophet who taught that it was acceptable to compromise with sin. However, he didn't start that way." Balak, the king of the Moabites asked Balaam, the prophet of God, to curse those who God blessed. King Balak wanted Balaam to curse Israel because "he saw all that Israel had done to the Amorites and Moab was sick with dread because of the children of Israel" (Numbers 22:2-6). Balaam received a word from God: "You shall not go with them; you shall not curse the people, for they are blessed" (Numbers 22:12). King Balak did not give up easily and offered to honor Balaam greatly. He tempted him with an offering to increase his pay.

> Cain's way was to get rid of his brother, God's Way was to change Cain's heart.

Balaam led Israel into idolatry and immorality: "Look, these women caused the children of Israel, through the counsel of Balaam, to trespass against the LORD in the incident of Peor, and there was a plague among the congregation of the LORD"

> Balaam led Israel into idolatry and immorality.

Chapter 2: Making the Adjustment

(Numbers 31:16). Even Jesus addressed this in Revelation: "But I have a few things against you, because you have there those who hold the doctrine of Balaam, who taught Balak to put a stumbling block before the children of Israel, to eat things sacrificed to idols, and to commit sexual immorality" (Revelation 2:14). Balaam did not rebel in ignorance but led the people in error because of his love of money.

Peter also addressed this in his second letter. "They have a heart trained in covetous practices, and are accursed children. They have forsaken the right way and gone astray, following the way of Balaam the son of Peor, who loved the wages of unrighteousness, but he was rebuked for his iniquity: a dumb donkey speaking with a man's voice restrained the madness of the prophet" (2 Peter 2:14-16). To some degree all believer's hearts are trained up by the world. But the Spirit within a believer trains up the heart to go God's

> **They have a heart trained in covetous practices.**

Way. This begins when a believer places Him first in his/her life. Balaam went astray and stepped into the idea that ministry was for making money instead of caring for God's people. People became a means to an end for Balaam. Balaam represents the apostate that would tamper with God's Will.

> *They soon forgot His works; they did not wait for His counsel, but lusted exceedingly in the wilderness, and tested God in the desert. And He gave them their request, but sent leanness into their soul.*
>
> **Psalm 106:13-15**

Pastor Josh stated,

> *In the apostate days of Jude, they are given over to their sensual desires. "You want this so bad, well here it is, but," God says, "in exchange I am going to give you leanness of soul." Oh friends, I want my soul to be strong. I want my soul to be able to handle whatever the enemy may tempt me with, as enticing as it may be. I want my soul to be strong in the day of trials and temptations. This requires a self-denial. It requires having a greater vision of who Jesus is in your*

life. It requires placing Jesus in His proper place in your heart. There is no room for idolatry if you desire a soul that is strong in Christ.

Jude's third warning is the rebellion of Korah. "Korah is one of the children of Israel. He rebelled against Moses' leadership when he told Moses, "You are taking on too much. We are all holy like you" (Numbers 16:1-35). Korah rebelled against God's Word by rebelling against the one God chose. What he really wanted was control. He wanted to lead in his own way. His heart was rebellious and had a non-submissive attitude that was arrogant and prideful. He was not satisfied where God had placed him. He wanted Moses' position. It really is best just to be where God planted you. It is futile to try to be something that God did not create you to be. This revolt was against God Himself.

> Korah rebelled against God's Word by rebelling against the one God chose.

God is a sovereign God Who raises leaders and can also cause them to fall. Korah tried to rise up against God, and God not only caused him to fall but also opened up the earth, swallowing up Korah and 250 other leaders.

Cain, Balaam, and Korah were greedy, unloving, and insubordinate to God's appointed leadership. False teachers are liable to undermine the faith of others just as hidden rocks can wreck a ship. They are shepherds who only look out for themselves. They promise much and deliver little. They make a lot of noise but do not have the lives to back up their words. The church family needs to watch the lives of those who claim to be teachers. God shepherds in a way that cares for His people. He gathers those who have been scattered and gives them peace.

At any point the three men that Jude used as examples could have made adjustments toward God. However, they all chose to go their own ways. They chose to follow their own pleasures. God gave His people an opportunity in Isaiah 58:13 to turn back to Him. In order for them to obey, they had to submit their hearts to His Ways. This requires training and a watchful eye.

Training the Heart

People's hearts have not changed since the fall of man in the garden. While it is easy to look at Jude's examples provided regarding apostates and think how bad they were, your heart has the same sinful condition. Your life in Christ will require making adjustments as God convicts you. When you refuse to adjust, you refuse to obey. The longer you disobey the further you fall into sin. Your heart will not naturally obey God unless you surrender it to Him. This requires learning His Ways. As long as you have idols in your life, you will not make the necessary adjustments in obedience.

An idol is any object that you choose to place your affection and worship in above your affection and worship for God. Cain's idol was himself because he desired to go his own way. Balaam's idol was money, and Korah's idol was position. These idols led to rebellion. When your heart is full of sin, your affection will be toward whatever fulfills your sinful desire.

Let's look a little further into these hearts not surrendered to God in order to gain insight into potential idols in your life.

1. A **hard heart** is merciless and cruel.
2. A **stiff-necked** heart will not bend to God's Way.
3. A **deceived** heart is easily led into error.
4. A **confused** heart cannot tell what is true and what is a lie.
5. A **proud** heart is focused on self.
6. A **rebellious** heart will not follow authority and will try to destroy it.

These characteristics describe the hearts of Cain, Balaam, and Korah. You may think that these do not apply to you because you are not a leader like these men. But even members of a church who are not in leadership are in danger of these characteristics. When your heart reflects these qualities you can easily be led into sin. As Pastor Josh stated, "I desire my soul to be strong in order to endure trials and temptations." If you have that same desire, then you will

> A surrendered heart will worship God alone.

need to allow the Lord to train your heart in His Way. This requires surrendering your heart to Him. A surrendered heart will worship God alone.

The qualities of a heart surrendered to the Lord:

1. A **willing** heart is pleased and desires to obey God.
2. A **glad** heart is cheerful and joyous toward God.
3. A **wise** heart with understanding can discern spiritual things and make correct judgments.
4. A heart with **integrity** has a pure moral character.
5. An **obedient** heart is submissive to authority and willing to yield.
6. A **pure and honest** heart is real, genuine, and faithful.

In order for you to have the right heart posture, you must surrender your heart to the Lord. When you do, He will grant you a new heart. This seems to be where many Christians lose understanding. It is not about making a hard heart better but it is about God granting you an entirely new heart. However, when you have idols in your life God does not have access to your heart. If the Israelites were to stop doing their pleasure on God's Holy Day, they needed to adjust to Him and get their heart back in order.

Training your heart consists of spending time in God's Word and learning how to hear from His Spirit. The goal is to obey as soon as you get a Word from God. Through this process God will provide you with everything that you need for life and godliness (see 2 Peter 1:3). Your life in Christ requires adjusting to God's direction. God gave Cain the opportunity to do that.

> *So the LORD said to Cain, "Why are you angry? And why has your countenance fallen? If you do well, will you not be accepted? And if you do not do well, sin lies at the door. And its desire is for you, but you should rule over it."*
> **Genesis 4:6-7**

Cain had the opportunity to surrender to God. If he had adjusted to God, then he would not have murdered Abel. Cain instead chose to follow his angry heart. God also provided Balaam with exact instructions

Chapter 2: Making the Adjustment

on how to respond to King Balak, but Balaam chose to follow the desire of his sinful heart. Korah also could have submitted to Moses' authority at any point before he was swallowed up by the earth, but he chose to follow the desire of his rebellious heart.

You will not live life on this side of heaven without sinning. However, if you learn to train your heart to be sensitive to the direction of the Holy Spirit, then God can intercept your heart at the start of sin rather than when you find yourself in deep bondage. As you allow the Spirit to train your heart in the Ways of God, you will be able to know exactly what the Lord is asking you to do. As you obey God and adjust your life to Him, your heart will grow in love for God. Just as applying horseback riding principles will improve your balance, applying God's principles will train your heart in the Spirit instead of the flesh. The more you fix your eyes ahead when you ride, the more natural that will become. It is important to have a watchful eye as a believer. This will be highly effective for the growth of the body of Christ.

The Watchful Eye

The Spirit of God was at work in the life of Balaam. When Balaam decided to saddle his donkey and follow the princes of Moab, God sent an angel to stand in Balaam's way. The donkey was able to see the angel, but Balaam did not. Balaam became angry with his donkey because the donkey laid down when she saw the angel. Balaam struck the donkey and God opened the mouth of the donkey to say, "What have I done to you, that you have struck me these three times" (see Numbers 22:22-28).

> *Then the LORD opened Balaam's eyes, and he saw the Angel of the LORD standing in the way with His drawn sword in His hand; and he bowed his head and fell flat on his face.*
> **Numbers 22:31**

When the Lord opened Balaam's eyes he saw spiritual things. Balaam did not know that the angel was in his way. There is much you can learn from this story. There are times in which the Spirit is blocking you from going the wrong way and you are unable to see

> God's Word provides spiritual eyesight when you surrender to His Way.

the spiritual reason. God's Word provides spiritual eyesight when you surrender to His Way. Without God's Spirit, you will not know which way to turn.

Many times when the Spirit is blocking something in your life, you may continue to pursue it anyway. This is disobedience. There will always be a truth that God knows that you are unaware of and by blocking you, He is protecting you. However, just like when riding a horse, your eyes can focus on the wrong thing. Because Balaam was focused on money and not God, he pushed past the Spirit's leading to go his own way.

God will provide you with everything you need to stay in right relationship with Him, even when you cannot see. This requires trust. When you are weak the Holy Spirit can take over for you.

> *Likewise the Spirit also helps in our weaknesses. For we do not know what we should pray for as we ought, but the Spirit Himself makes intercession for us with groanings which cannot be uttered.*
>
> **Romans 8:26**

The Holy Spirit will help you in your weakness from an internal relationship. His help for you does not come from the outside. He is present and active in your heart. The Holy Spirit knows if you love God because He lives within and searches your heart.

For example, suppose you know you should move somewhere to do the work of ministry but things on this earth are not cooperating. The Spirit within searches your heart and gives you the hope you need that it will come to pass. You do not know exactly how to pray, but the Spirit searches your heart and gives you what you need to overcome weaknesses. The result is that you live and work as though it is already done. All you are waiting for is timing. The Spirit makes intercession for us from the internal and the result is peace and hopeful anticipation. When the Spirit works in your heart, words are not enough to express your deepest feelings of God's initiative in your life. Most

> As the Spirit makes intercession for us from the internal the result is peace and hopeful anticipation.

often, the love of God through your life can express itself more in a look, a hug, or a touch. When the Spirit is speaking to you and through you, it cannot be contained or expressed completely.

This should be the experience of all Christians. But the flesh wars against the Spirit. Too often the believer is not walking in the Spirit and does not experience this inner wisdom of the Spirit. It seems that believers have lost the ability to depend on the Spirit. If you are not in fellowship with God, then you will not hear these wordless messages. In this sense, the Spirit has been quenched.

But when you walk in the Spirit, the Spirit takes your sincere prayers and helps you make sense of what is next and how you should continue to pray. When God works in the areas you have been waiting on Him for, an overwhelming trust washes over you. The struggle makes the promise extra special. A surrendered heart that walks with God daily will begin to see circumstances and situations with spiritual eyesight. When the Lord prepares your heart for years and finally brings the promise to pass you see it through years of spiritual preparation. There is great rest in releasing your heart to the Lord. A watchful eye is able to continue in this rest by recognizing what is of God and what is not of God. As long as you cannot see what is of God, you are open to doing your pleasure on His Holy Day. When this happens you will lose spiritual rest.

> The struggle makes the promise extra special.

> There is great rest in releasing your heart to the Lord.

Riding on High Hills

Riding on High Hills Devotion Chapter 2

Making the Adjustment

"... From doing your pleasure on My Holy day..."
Isaiah 58:13

Just as the focus of the eye is important in horseback riding, it is also important in your spiritual life. In order for you to make the adjustment from doing your pleasure on the Lord's Holy Day, your heart's desire will have to change. As your desire changes, your spiritual eyesight will begin to develop. In horseback riding if you notice that your eye is looking down, then you must adjust to the proper position. You may need to do this several times as you are learning. This is also true for spiritual eyesight. The minute that you notice that you have taken your eyes off of Jesus, you must make the adjustment through repentance and surrender. To keep your eyes on Jesus means to keep your eyes set on His Word and His Spirit to guide your every step. You must focus on what God is leading you to and not what He is leading you from.

> **You must focus on what God is leading you to and not what He is leading you from.**

My eyes are ever toward the LORD, for He shall pluck my feet out of the net.
Psalm 25:15

Imagine walking through the forest along a path that is not well defined. Staying on the path would be your focus, lest you step into a hole or become disoriented and lost. If you knew that there were many animal traps set, it would make you even more alert and cautious. Knowing this, instead of taking a relaxing walk, your concern would be to scope out the area and make sure that you avoid those traps! Learning to scope out and avoid traps can be quite exhausting. Your mind, emotions, and body become highly alert, knowing you can still miss a trap and become ensnared.

Satan has set many traps for God's people. His traps tend to be highly camouflaged. How would you avoid these traps? Do you avoid them by consciously and carefully watching for each trap? If so, then the whole of your Christian life would be on the defensive. This passage reveals that if you keep your eyes toward the Lord, you will always be on a path that avoids traps.

Your salvation is not in your ability to avoid traps but in your total trust in the Lord. If you trust Him enough to keep your focus on Him only, He will pluck your feet out of the trap. Your focus should not be on developing skills to avoid traps but on keeping your eyes on Jesus Christ Himself! The Scripture states, He must increase, but I must decrease" (John 3:30). As you rely more on Jesus to develop you, you will rely less on your own efforts. This is the surrendered life!

> Your salvation is not in your ability to avoid traps, but in your total trust in the Lord.

As your eyes stay focused on Jesus, you look forward to seeing the fullness of life that is ahead. Now, you can focus on the big picture and see the forest and its beauty. Instead of looking down trying to find traps, your eyes follow Christ, and He keeps you free from the trap.

THE HEART'S POSTURE #2
Learn to keep your eyes up, always fixed on Jesus. The longer you do, the greater your spiritual eyesight will become.

THE RIDER'S POSITION #2
Keep your eyes focused on where you are going.

Chapter 2: Making the Adjustment

Riding on High Hills

Riding Principle #3

Body Position: Light Hands and Strong Legs

Now that you have set your foundation and see where you are heading, you need to give the horse direction. This is accomplished through leg pressure and light hand guidance. Your legs not only guide the horse but also ask the horse to pick up different gaits. The gaits include walking, trotting, cantering, and galloping. Your hands are used to guide the reins, which are connected to the bit. To ask the horse to move forward you place your hands forward and to ask them to slow down or stop you pull the reins backward. However, the hands work in connection to the rest of your body. You can technically stop the horse with your body alone, but not all horses are trained to be that sensitive to your body. Therefore, the reins are an added guide.

Your reins should never be tight in the horse's mouth. This creates a lot of tension and is very uncomfortable to the horse. Many times a new rider tries to balance with his hands and squeezes his legs for stability, but this is telling the horse to stop with the hands and to go with the legs. This confuses the horse and frustrates the rider. This is why it is important to establish balance and a solid foundation before asking the horse to do harder tasks in riding. It is also important to note that your hands can be connected to the bit without being in the horses mouth (being heavy-handed). When you have a proper connection the horse's mouth will foam. This is a good sign.

You also need to learn where to place your leg to ask for what you are desiring the horse to accomplish. To move the horse's body to the left you will need to apply your right leg and open up your left rein. Think about the unmoving hand and strong leg as a barrier where you do not want the horse to go and the open rein and leg as the place where you would like them to go. Remember that horses move away from pressure. The goal is to use

> When he/she submits to the pressure then the rider needs to release the pressure and it is in this moment that the horse and rider find connection and delight.

your leg to push the horse onto the bit. When this happens the horse is carrying his own body and this creates a supple, balanced, and comfortable horse to ride. The horse has to find the release of pressure, and he is happy when he does. When he/she submits to the pressure, the rider should release the pressure. In this moment, the horse and rider find connection and delight.

Chapter 3
Finding Rest in the Release

"...And call the Sabbath a delight.."
Isaiah 58:13

Once you have established a solid foundation in Christ and are able to see spiritual things, you begin to recognize the guidance of the Holy Spirit in your life. This direction is directly related to your daily relationship with God through love and obedience. When Christ establishes your heart you are prepared to do what He calls you to do. As long as you stay connected to Him you will find rest in your journey. If you recognize that there is something in your life blocking you from this rest, then release it. When you release it you will find rest in Him.

The Israelites were not releasing their way to follow God's Way. Therefore, they were not at peace with God. You have been learning the desire of God's heart toward the Israelites through Isaiah 58:13. He wanted them to stop trampling on the Sabbath, turn from their way, and call the Sabbath a delight. Not only were they going their own way, but they were also using the disguise of religion.

> *Yet they seek Me daily, and delight to know My ways, as a nation that did righteousness, and did not forsake the ordinance of their God. They ask of Me the ordinances of justice; they take delight in approaching God. "Why have we fasted,' they say, "and You have not seen? Why have we afflicted our souls, and You take no notice?' 'In fact, in the day of your fast you find pleasure, and*

exploit all your laborers. Indeed you fast for strife and debate, and to strike with the fist of wickedness. You will not fast as you do this day, to make your voice heard on high.
Isaiah 58:2-4

The Israelites were participating in religious activity, but only for selfish gain. In their arrogance and pride, they were frustrated at God for not recognizing that they were fasting. God responded that they were fasting out of strife and debate. In verse 5 He said, "Is it a fast that I have chosen, a day for a man to afflict his soul?" They were using fasting to exploit their laborers and get what they wanted from the people. Their flesh had become their god. God responded to let them know the purpose of His fast.

> Their flesh had become their god.

Is this not the fast that I have chosen: to loose the bonds of wickedness, to undo the heavy burdens, to let the oppressed go free, and that you break every yoke? Is it not to share your bread with the hungry, and that you bring to your house the poor who are cast out; when you see the naked, that you cover him, and not hide yourself from your own flesh?
Isaiah 58:6-7

There is no delight found in this type of man-made religion. When the leaders control God's people by using His Ways for their own personal gain, there is no delight. This is evil. Many leaders continue to do this today. They use God's ordained practices for their own gain. It is extremely dangerous to use God's Way with a heart full of selfish desires. This is pushing people out of church and away from God. There are so many people who have a story regarding "church hurt." Jesus was also treated poorly by religious leaders, but they did not sway Him from His purpose. If you have been treated poorly in church, do not let it keep you from delighting in the Lord. God will not take treating other people poorly lightly. These people can draw you in but, as you get close they will reveal their true colors. The key is to cling tightly to Jesus and hold loosely to people.

> The key is to cling tightly to Jesus and hold loosely to people.

It is nearly impossible to know the state of another person's heart. You can observe other people's lives to see if they have spiritual fruit, but sometimes people are good at acting and can fool you into thinking they love God when they actually are only pretending. This is why it is better to hold loosely to people. Jude felt strongly about exposing these people. While the book of Jude may seem as negative because of Jude's heavy correction, the truth is that God's Way is conditional. In order for you to find delight and joy, you must recognize the negative in your own heart. To arrive at the promise that God has for you, you must recognize that there is no good news without exposing bad news. This is because the world is full of evil and sin. God, however, desires to bless His people. The blessings come to those who choose God's Way through His Spirit.

The Sabbath was created by God for His people. Therefore, His people should honor the Sabbath as a gift. The spiritual work on the Sabbath is a delight to a heart surrendered to Christ. But God's people have drifted from God's desire for the Sabbath make it a drudgery instead of a delight. The Sabbath has become a contest as to what ministry or program can bring the most people. Many have lost sight of what is of God and what is not of God. Just because someone looks like they are on your team, does not mean that they are. You will know who is truly surrendered to Christ when they receive a rebuke from Him. The way someone responds to a rebuke reveals the condition of the person's heart. Spiritual correction is almost completely lost in churches today because few are qualified to see what needs to be corrected (see Galatians 6:1). Many Christians call others *godly* but use this term loosely and incorrectly. When someone is deceptive and treating others poorly, they are not godly. When you cannot have an honest conversation with someone to resolve conflict, he is not godly. Christians need to be cautious when call-

> The spiritual work on the Sabbath is a delight to a heart surrendered to Christ.

> Just because someone looks like they are on your team, does not mean that they are.

ing others godly. It would be better if Christians stopped calling people godly and just focused on God.

Pastor Josh stated in his sermon on the book of Jude, "It is a painful thing when you assume someone is on the team, but was never on the team in his heart." He is talking about people who creep into the church and act as though they are believers but are not. These people are not Christians, but they can fool you into thinking they are by their words and actions. But what happens when you rebuke them? This is the real test. This is a good question to ask yourself, "How do you respond when Christ rebukes you?"

> It is a painful thing when you assume someone is on the team, but was never on the team in his heart.

In Isaiah 58, the people were doing what they wanted and claiming that it was of God. But God was saying that was not what He wanted. People want to delight in the Lord without following His Way. That will never happen. The way of sin does not bring delight. God's Way leads to redemption, but going your own way leads to rebuke.

> People want to delight in the Lord without following His Way.

Pastor Josh put it this way:

The word "apostate" means departing or wandering from the truth. The book of Jude discusses apostates in Israel who fell away by their unbelief. Then Jude draws our attention to the angels who were apostatized by the fact that they rebelled. Lastly, Jude reminds us of Sodom and Gomorrah and their apostasy caused by sexual immorality. In Jude 8, the truth is revealed that these dreamers, or some translations say these people, rely on their dreams, defile the flesh, and speak evil of dignitaries.

God judges rebellion. Jude's greatest emphasis was against those who reject the Lordship of Jesus Christ. These so-called leaders battled their own ungodly sexual desires. Ultimately because they rejected

Chapter 3: Finding Rest in the Release

God's authority over their lives, chose their own way, and spoke evil of anything that did not agree with their thinking.

Today, many choose the way of these dreamers. They think up ways that their own desires acceptable. They must reject God's law to be settled with their own law. This way of thinking is so dangerous that it leads people to eternal damnation. Once someone rejects God's authority, his mind gives way to godless thinking. In fact, the longer a person lives in this state, the less likely it is for him to ever repent and return to the Ways of God. He thinks his way is acceptable because he enjoys what his way gets him. This is the result of inner deception.

It is sad to think of the outcome of the lives of these violators of truth. Paul said, "Therefore God also gave them up to uncleanness, in the lusts of their hearts, to dishonor their bodies among themselves, who exchanged the truth of God for the lie, and worshiped and served the creature rather than the Creator" (Romans 1:24-25).

God rebukes all false teachers. If a person is not born of God and walking in His Spirit, then he will turn naturally to his own thinking for guidance. That is what is happening with so many in the church today. People join the church on a profession of faith but never had a born-again experience. Then, they get in leadership roles and begin to teach. They do not make sense spiritually but set a precedent for many others to be in church without the church being in them.

> **God rebukes all false teachers.**

Pastor Josh went on,

> *These dreamers are ones that say they have a new dream and that they are new evangelicals. God speaks through His Word, but these people claim a new vision, a new morality. They have a new dream relying on their own visions and claim that they can live any way that they please. This mindset rejects God's authority. They see themselves as the sole authority and would never rely on the Word of God. They unhitch themselves from the Old Testament and make claims that those living in sin have more faith than true believers. The problem is that this type of thinking is a complete lie.*

The truth is that Jesus is the fulfillment of the Old Testament. The Old Testament predicted that the Messiah would come, die, be buried, and would rise. This is the way that Jesus is presented in the New Testament. And as the Christ, the Messiah, the Scripture tells us Jesus is coming back for His own. You must see that, as a believer, the Word of God is the very authority of your life.

You will never find rest going your own way, and you will never delight in the Sabbath as long as flesh is your god. God's command is to have no other gods but Him. Until you submit and acknowledge God in His proper place, you will not rest, and you certainly will not find delight in the Sabbath. Flesh is always scheming to find a way to get ahead. This type of life is exhausting. When you release your way to God's Way, you will have rest.

Flesh is a god

Remember that in order to keep the Sabbath day holy, you must follow the three commands that precede it. Those who are going their own way and claiming that they are going God's Way are actually placing their flesh on the throne. You will find this often when discussing God's people in the Old Testament. God said, "You shall have no other gods before Me" (Exodus 20:3). Instead, His people acted religious outwardly and hated God inwardly for not rewarding them (see Isaiah 58:1-5). You will never delight in God as long as your actions are not in line with God's Word. Delight requires a pure heart that takes flesh off of the throne and places God in His proper place. When you do this, you begin to delight in your relationship with Jesus. Through this love relationship He will guide and direct you on what He desires.

> Delight requires a pure heart that takes flesh off of the throne and places God in His proper place.

Jeremiah also faced apostates and God's chosen people following their own way.

> *"Therefore behold, I am against the prophets," says the LORD, "who steal My words every one from his neighbor. Behold, I am*

against the prophets," says the LORD, "who use their tongues and say, 'He says.' Behold, I am against those who prophesy false dreams," says the LORD, "and tell them, and cause My people to err by their lies and by their recklessness. Yet I did not send them or command them; therefore they shall not profit this people at all," says the LORD. "So when these people or the prophet or the priest ask you, saying, 'What is the oracle of the LORD?' you shall then say to them, 'What oracle?' I will even forsake you," says the LORD. "And as for the prophet and the priest and the people who say, 'The oracle of the LORD!' I will even punish that man and his house. Thus every one of you shall say to his neighbor, and every one to his brother, 'What has the LORD answered?' and, 'What has the LORD spoken?' And the oracle of the LORD you shall mention no more. For every man's word will be his oracle, for you have perverted the words of the living God, the LORD of hosts, our God. Thus you shall say to the prophet, "What has the LORD answered you?' and, 'What has the LORD spoken?'

Jeremiah 23:30-37

God informed Jeremiah about what to say to these false teachers who claimed they were speaking the oracles of God when God never told them anything. This is a clear picture of what happens when flesh becomes a god. No one is exempt from losing fellowship with Jesus. The moment flesh becomes a god in your heart, you will go your own way. Deception may even blind you from what you are doing. It begins with one act of disobedience in your relationship with Christ and ends with a complete disconnect from the One you enjoyed. You will begin to notice a lack of love, joy, and peace, but will still try to convince yourself you are going God's Way. Jesus says, "Apart from Me you can do nothing" (John 15:5). Breaking fellowship with Jesus is detrimental to your spiritual life. While you may look like you are doing great work for God, in fact, you will only be following your own desires. This is dangerous because this is blasphemy.

> Breaking fellowship with Jesus is detrimental to your spiritual life.

Pastor Josh also noted,

> *It is powerful and sobering to think about our great Savior as the great Destroyer. In verse 5, Jude wrote, "But I want to remind you, though you once knew this, that the Lord, having saved the people out of the land of Egypt, afterward destroyed those who did not believe." In verse 6, Jude writes about "the fallen angels, that He has reserved in everlasting chains under darkness for the judgment of that great day." In verse 7, he wrote about "Sodom and Gomorrah, and the cities around them in a similar manner to these, having given themselves over to sexual immorality and gone after strange flesh, are set forth as an example, suffering the vengeance of eternal fire." Then in verse 10, Jude wrote about how these people blasphemed against anything they did not understand.*
>
> *Many think of blasphemy as taking the Lord's name in vain. However it is important to recognize that blasphemy is deeper than that. As a believer you blaspheme the Lord when you do not do what He asks. Blasphemy sounds like this: "I understand what the Word of God says, but I'm not going to do that." Another example is, "I understand that the Word of God tells me not to cohabitate and have sex with someone that's not my spouse, but I'm not going to listen to that," or, "I understand that the Word of God tells me not to be a drunkard, but I'm not going to listen to that." It is knowing God's Word, having His Spirit dwell in you, and then completely disobeying Him.*

> **As a believer you blaspheme the Lord when you do not do what He asks.**

God's people were performing God's Way outwardly but inwardly were rejecting Him. They claimed Him with their words but despised Him in their hearts. This is what Isaiah and Jeremiah were facing, and it is what the church still faces today. The sinful heart that the prophets and disciples faced in biblical times is the same sinful heart in people today. Many try to teach that the times are different and so the church must change its approach. This is false. Society may look different, but the human condition is the same. The church should never change the preaching of the Lord Jesus Christ. Make no mistake, those who blaspheme God will be judged. Jesus is the Head of the Church. If the church is to find rest, it must follow the Will and Way of Christ.

The Head is Your Rest

> *So let no one judge you in food or in drink, or regarding a festival or a new moon or sabbaths, which are a shadow of things to come, but the substance is of Christ.*
> **Colossians 2:16-17**

Jesus did not come to destroy the law or the prophets but to fulfill the law (see Matthew 5:17). This truth reveals that Jesus is the Sabbath. God designed the ten commandments to keep believers in right relationship with Him, but according to Paul they were only *a shadow of things to come.* The law pointed to the coming of Jesus. Through Jesus' death and resurrection the law was fulfilled and the debt was paid. Therefore, to keep in right relationship with God requires you to be in right relationship with Jesus. You do this by submitting your life to Him and walking with Him daily. The Sabbath day will still be observed but with Jesus as the center instead of rules. This makes Jesus your rest.

> *Come to Me, all you who labor and are heavy laden, and I will give you rest. Take My yoke upon you and learn from Me, for I am gentle and lowly in heart, and you will find rest for your souls. For My yoke is easy and My burden is light.*
> **Matthew 11:28-30**

Jesus is the Lord of the Sabbath (see Matthew 12:8). He is the Spirit of the whole law. When you walk with Him, your desire will be to attend church in order to worship the Lord, the One that you love. Attending

> **Attending church without a relationship with Jesus will not produce rest, because rest is found in Christ not in church.**

church without a relationship with Jesus will not produce rest, because rest is found in Christ not in church. It is true that you can find Christ in church through other believers and the reading of the Word, but until you come to Him in a personal relationship you will not find rest for your soul. You must release your life to Him to find the rest that He offers.

Judaism was a mixture of Jewish religion and Christianity. The false teaching portrayed that obeying the Old Testament laws was equal to salvation. Paul stated that these things were "a shadow of things to come, but the substance is of Christ" (Colossians 2:17). The challenge for many of the converted Jews to Christianity was whether the converted Gentiles needed to practice their Jewish ways. Paul was teaching them that Christ was enough! A light behind a person casts a shadow and the shadow goes before that person showing him the way. Nothing should be taken away from the Old Testament. The Old Testament cast a shadow on what was to come. It is the beginning of the story of Christ. Everything in the Old Testament pointed to the coming of Christ. Many Jewish customs were not destroyed but they were also not part of salvation. They could be a custom that reminded the Jews who had become Christians of what was to come.

There are those who put a lot of thought into angels, visions, and dreams. They equate their experiences and their thinking with truth. Just because you are a believer and can think does not mean it is biblical thinking. It is more appropriate to focus on the clear Word of God in Scripture than to try and understand your own thinking. Holding on to Christ nourishes your heart and mind to grow in the Lord. You will not hold on to Christ if you have a high view of yourself. Your intellectual thinking can take you away from God instead of toward Him. That is why Paul states that you will be cheated of your reward if you do not hold fast to Christ's instructions with true humility (see Colossians 2:18).

> Just because you are a believer and can think does not mean it is biblical thinking.

Since Christ is the Head of the body, all direction for truth and life should come from Him. The moment you start living by anything you claim as truth that is not clearly revealed in Scripture, you will be thrown off course. Christ must increase and you must decrease. Christ must have preeminence in your heart and mind. If He does not, then you are susceptible to error. When Christ is first in your life and in the lives of those around you, Christ's Presence brings unity. As each member of the body becomes spiritually healthy, the body grows into Christ-likeness. Any unhealthy member brings harm to the rest of the body.

Chapter 3: Finding Rest in the Release

Growth increase comes from God as the body works together in following Christ. One's preferences, individuality, and desires will not accomplish unity. God's Spirit grows the body into the Head. The church does not increase simply because of abilities, money, and organization. What should the church do?

> *Rest in the LORD, and wait patiently for Him...*
> **Psalm 37:7**

Call the Sabbath a Delight

Until your heart enters into a personal relationship with Jesus, you will not be ready to become a leader in the body. As your heart is established and secured in Jesus, you are able to follow His Way for the church instead of your own way. If you have yet to find delight in your relationship with Christ, the Sabbath will not be a delight but an obligation. Many leaders in church have lost their way in regard to their walk with God. Because of this their role is just a job to them. This is killing the body of Christ. If you realize that you have no delight in Christ and have been living your life the wrong way, take some time to either receive Christ for the first time or to return to your relationship with Him through repentance.

> *If you have yet to find delight in your relationship with Christ, the Sabbath will not be a delight but an obligation.*

If you have ever experienced delight in Christ and now recognize that you have lost all joy, then you most likely have stepped out of fellowship with Jesus. Jesus came to give life. Everything about your life in Christ should bring great joy and delight. This includes attending church and obeying God's assignments. If you are not doing these things, then something is wrong in your relationship with Jesus.

> *Everything about your life in Christ should bring great joy and delight.*

The same is true in horseback riding. As you are learning to ride, you may become frustrated by a difficult task because you want the process to move ahead. This mindset kills your relationship with your horse, and the same mind-set in Christianity kills your relationship with Jesus. You begin to worship the goal instead of Jesus. You will never find delight for your soul by accomplishing goals in your life. Delight for your soul only comes in your love relationship with Jesus. If you cannot call the Sabbath a delight, then you have shifted your focus off of Christ and onto accomplishing a goal. In order for your position in the saddle to become automatic, you must not only learn the riding principle, but also you must learn to listen to your horse. The same is true in your walk with God. In order to have a secure heart posture, you must not only learn God's commands, but also learn to listen to and obey Jesus through a love relationship.

Chapter 3: Finding Rest in the Release

Riding on High Hills Devotion Chapter 3

Finding Rest in the Release

"...And call the Sabbath a delight.."
Isaiah 58:13

Just as your hands and legs provide your horse with direction, Jesus provides direction to your life through His Word and His Spirit. When you are in obedience to Christ, then you will be at rest. When you place leg pressure on your horse and he moves in the right direction, you release the pressure and your horse finds rest. But when you place leg pressure on the horse and he does not move in the right direction, you increase the pressure. This creates a lack of connection between horse and rider. One scenario represents obedience, and the other represents disobedience. When Jesus places pressure on your life to move in a certain direction and you do not obey, you will experience increased pressure. This brings disunity and there is no delight in disunity.

> Just as your hands and legs provide your horse with direction, Jesus provides direction to your life through His Word and His Spirit.

God desires for your heart to be at rest. Otherwise He would not have established a day of rest. Refraining from physical labor does not necessarily mean your heart will be at rest. There are two types of rest, physical and spiritual. This is where many misinterpret the purpose of the Sabbath. The Jewish leaders focused solely on physical rest and enforced it with a hard and oppressive hand. You can stop all physical labor on the Lord's day and feel more stressed out than before. When you stop activity, God reveals the reality of your heart.

There is only one way to honestly call the Sabbath a delight and that is through a heart that loves Jesus. Otherwise, the Sabbath just represents something that you have to do, and it becomes works-based instead of faith-based. Your heart is the key. Jesus is the Lord of the Sabbath and He will guide you every step of the way in your Christian life. As He guides, you must obey Him and through obedience you will find delight. This establishes a connection that you will never want to lose. In horseback riding, you help your horse find delight by keeping your hands light and your legs strong and making it clear what you are asking. A heavy hand produces an unhappy horse. This principle can be applied spiritually as well. Remember that your hands connect to the horse's mouth and if you are heavy handed then you are forcing instead of guiding. Jesus does not force, He guides with love. As He guides you in your life, you must learn to hold tightly to Him and loosely to anything that He desires for you to release. Remember there is rest in the release. As you release the things of life in your heart that weigh you down and allow Jesus to take the reins of your heart, you will find rest and great delight in your relationship with Christ.

> There is only one way to honestly call the Sabbath a delight and that is through a heart that loves Jesus.

> Jesus does not force, He guides with love.

THE HEART'S POSTURE #3
Stand firm in your relationship with Christ and release all things that can break your connection with Him.

THE RIDER'S POSITION #3
Light hands and strong legs produce clear communication to the horse. This clarity allows the horse to find rest as it obeys.

Section Two:

The Church's Posture

Chapter 4: Honor through Submission

Riding Principle #4

Honor the Horse

We have been focusing on your body position as a rider. Now we shift to the horse. Much like people, horses have different personalities and training levels. It is important to honor each horse you encounter. In order to honor the horse you must learn that horse's personality and level of training.

While horses are obviously different than people, some aspects of their personalities are similar to people's personalities. For example, horses can be introverted or extroverted. Extroverted horses are very curious and tend to get into things. They can be really funny but also annoying. They tend to show their expressions on the outside. Introverted horses are quite different. Their expressions are on the inside, and they tend to be much less curious. The danger with an introverted horse is that they can bottle up their frustrations and explode instead of providing clear cues to the rider.

Another aspect of a horse's personality is confidence. Some horses are confident and some are more insecure and fearful. While confidence can increase through training, some horses are more fearful than others. A fearful horse does not need an inexperienced rider. This can be a dangerous combination.

Training is another aspect to consider when learning to honor the horse. It is not honorable to expect a horse to perform past its training abilities, just as much as it is not honorable to expect a rider to perform past his abilities. As a complete beginner the best training level for a horse is a schoolmaster. Schoolmasters teach beginners how to ride. They are reliable, trustworthy, and knowledgeable horses. These horses allow the rider to make mistakes without causing a dangerous situation. Schoolmaster horses teach you to ride correctly.

The next level of a trained horse would be a finished horse. These types of horses know their jobs and do not need constant practice. However, not all finished horses are schoolmasters. A horse that is finished is versatile and can adjust but may not always necessarily teach a rider how to ride. Some finished horses may not be suitable for an inexperienced rider because they may be faster and stronger than a new rider can handle.

There are also horses that have started in training but are not yet finished. These horses require more practice but have the basic solid foundation to know what the rider is asking.

Lastly, you have green horses which are just beginning their training. You may hear a person say that a horse is *green broke*. This means that they have had a rider on their back, but they are not trained beyond that. Much like the rider each horse needs to begin with a solid training foundation.

> Honoring the horse means getting to know the animal and respecting their personality and training level.

Honoring the horse means getting to know the animal and respecting their personality and training level.

Chapter 4
Honor through Submission

"The holy day of the LORD honorable, and shall honor Him, not doing your own ways..."
Isaiah 58:13

It is amazing how God connects people through shared interests. It is also unusual to find people who love both God and horses. God did just that by connecting Pastor Josh with *Think Lifechange/Victory Reins* ministry. Pastor Josh shares his testimony of how he came to know and love horses:

> *I was introduced to horses in 2011 at Windy Hill Farm in Millersburg, Ohio. Ted and Kathy DeHass were the first to show me what it means to be a horseman. I have admired horses but needed to finish my theological training before taking on a new hobby. In 2018, I had just completed my Doctorate, and the Director of the Ministry program at Gateway Seminary, Dr. Jim Wilson, asked me what I planned to do after graduation. I knew the answer immediately: horsemanship. At that point, I had ridden a horse one time in 2011 at Windy Hill farm.*
>
> *I began researching barns near me and looking up different ministries using horses. I noticed an equestrian ministry in Texas, liked their Facebook page, and moved on. I began looking around our community to see how I could be around horses. I learned quickly that horses and affordability are not synonymous. So I began to look for any way to volun-*

teer. I volunteered at the Calvin Center in Woolsey, Georgia to practice more of the basics of horsemanship and helping special needs children.

I signed up for riding lessons with my oldest daughter, Chloe, at Step-N-Free Stables in Fayetteville, Georgia. So, at the ripe age of 34, I, as the Billy Madison prototype, showed up at the barn with my daughter and other ten and twelve-year-old girls to learn how to ride. I am grateful for Stephanie Free and Jennifer Powell's generosity, who showed us patience. Jennifer challenged us to love, understand, and respect the horse.

As I was beginning to learn, God brought several other people into my life, like World Champion trainer Lew Sterrett of Sermon on the Mount ministries. Lew is the kind of cowboy you immediately respect. He oozes coolness and confidence. I gravitated toward him to learn more. I still do because I admire him and his unwavering faith in Christ and commitment to capturing the hearts of horses.

One afternoon, I was sitting in my office, and a counseling ministry stopped by for a meet and greet named Think LifeChange/Victory Reins. As we got acquainted, I was shocked to learn this was the same ministry I followed from Texas! I could see the Lord's hand in our meeting. I received their message and wanted our church to become partners with them. Shortly after our meeting, I attended a Think LifeChange/Victory Reins retreat, and God tenderly dealt with my unrepentant heart in several areas. He used the horses to show me physically what was happening in my spirit. I am forever grateful for what transpired at the retreat because I understood my need for repentance and how it is an excellent gift to the believer. I learned practical ways to keep my heart and mind clean and clear before the Lord.

> I could see the Lord's hand in our meeting... I learned practical ways to keep my heart and mind clean and clear before the Lord.

Mrs. Diane Rajani, the owner of Cedar Ridge Ranch, taught me to ride. I owe so much to Mrs. Diane. She is a superb horseman *and a gifted trainer. She would receive horses from around the country that were 'sticky' in areas and smooth out whatever trouble they had. Then, she would tell me, "Josh, get on!" She wanted to see how the horses would respond to a novice rider like myself. Sometimes, it worked very well. Other times, I ended up with some bumps and bruises. But as she would say, "If you want to be a cowboy, that's what it takes." I earned a few cowboy hats along my journey, but I was learning much more than horsemanship. I was learning leadership principles, grit, communication skills, patience, and love. The horses became my teachers, revealing things within my own heart.*

After a couple of years under Mrs. Diane's leadership, I was ready to purchase my own horse. Think LifeChange/ Victory Reins introduced me to John and Roslyn Boren of Shadow Rock Arena and this is where I purchased my horse Joe. The Borens are incredibly generous with their time and talent. Both are tremendous horse riders and deeply love people and the Lord. They have great faith, and I admire them immensely.

I am young in my horsemanship journey. I am committed to continued learning because of how God uses horses in my life. I see a direct reflection of my life and leadership through horses.

The Horse

Everyone who reads this book will not have a love of horses, but, there is still much horses can teach us about honor. The Bible mentions a specific type of horse: a *warhorse*. Warhorses provided armies additional strength in battles. These animals were large and full of power. In general, horses have incredible power and strength far exceeding human abilities. It is nearly impossible to pride yourself in your physical strength when you are standing next to a horse. For this reason, horses deserve honor. God created the horse as a helper for people, just as He created the Sabbath as a rest day for people. When you honor the horse, you honor the Creator.

> When you honor the horse, you honor the Creator.

Have you given the horse strength? Have you clothed his neck with thunder? Can you frighten him like a locust? His majestic snorting strikes terror. He paws in the valley, and rejoices in his strength; He gallops into the clash of arms. He mocks at fear, and is not frightened; Nor does he turn back from the sword. The quiver rattles against him, The glittering spear and javelin. He devours the distance with fierceness and rage; Nor does he come to a halt because the trumpet has sounded. At the blast of the trumpet he says, "Aha!" He smells the battle from afar, the thunder of captains and shouting.

Job 39:19-25

This passage describes the horse's strength. This horse was prepared and ready to engage in battle without fear. This is a different picture than how many use horses today. Many horse owners today have domesticated horses so much that they are not prepared for danger. While horses are strong and powerful, they are prey animals by nature. To rush into battle, a horse requires confidence. While some horses have more confidence than others, the horse also can receive confidence from its rider.

If you were to take an insecure horse into battle it would seem more dangerous than not having a horse at all because fear drives the horse more than the rider. Insecure horses are still physically powerful and strong, but their minds are fearful. Because fearful horses are more disobedient, they are more dangerous to riders. If the horse allows its mind to control its action instead of its rider, then the horse may hesitate or stop pursuing the battle. This is a prime opportunity for the enemy to strike. The horse needs to trust the rider just as the church needs to trust God.

> The horse needs to trust the rider just as the church needs to trust God... The strength that the church exhibits resides in the Holy Spirit alone.

The church is the body of Christ. The strength that the church exhibits resides in the Holy Spirit alone. Therefore, if the church decides to follow anyone other than the Head, Jesus, they will be weakened in spirit. The church has a much greater power than the horse, because it has the power of the Holy Spirit.

Consider a body of believers who have their hearts right with the Lord. Such a body would be prepared for spiritual battles and spiritual blessings. The horse is trained up to partner with the rider as an extension of the rider's body. The same is true of the church's relationship with Christ. If the church is trained up in the love of God, then it becomes a working body. But how do we accomplish this?

The Church's Posture

In Isaiah 58, God corrected the Israelites because they were using God's Way as a means to get their own way. Through this deception they complained that God was not noticing what they were doing (see Isaiah 58:1-14). Any church can fall into the trap of calling their own way, God's Way. In fact, many churches are doing this today by doing God's work by the power of their flesh. As long as you walk in the flesh, you will not properly serve the Lord. Your service will be based upon your own thinking and understanding rather than the direction that only Christ can provide.

In the book of Ephesians, Paul writes:

> *And walk in love, as Christ also has loved us and given Himself for us, an offering and a sacrifice to God for a sweet-smelling aroma.*
>
> **Ephesians 5:2**

Love is a fruit of the Spirit of God (see Galatians 5:22). You walk in the Love of God through the Spirit and a relationship with Jesus which requires life-long training in the Ways of God. In every situation that the church encounters, God has a Way that is pleasing to Him. If every leader and member of the church can learn how to walk in the Ways of God, then the church would be in complete unity. While this may not be realistic on earth, it is the ultimate goal of the church is to train and disciple God's people to walk in His Love. This training will not be without spiritual warfare. There will be people who come in to destroy

> You walk in the Love of God through the Spirit and a relationship with Jesus which requires life-long training in the Ways of God.

God's church. This is what the book of Jude warns against. It is critical to be aware of the types of people who attempt to destroy the church.

The book of Jude describes these types of people in the church:

> *These are grumblers, complainers, walking according to their own lusts; and they mouth great swelling words, flattering people to gain advantage. But you, beloved, remember the words which were spoken before by the apostles of our Lord Jesus Christ: how they told you that there would be mockers in the last time who would walk according to their own ungodly lusts. These are sensual persons, who cause divisions, not having the Spirit.*
> **Jude 1:16-19**

The people Jude described sinned against God in word and in action. He stated that they were:

1. **Grumblers and complainers**. This is one way you can sin with your mouth. The complaining comes from the heart but is revealed through words. Complaints are not always wrong; they can correct sin. Jude was referring to the sin of complaining. He referenced the children of Israel grumbling in the desert and explained that ultimately they were dissatisfied with God. They complained of their situation with harsh words against God.

2. **Those filled with lust of their own desires**. These people desired something that was forbidden and lusted after things and others.

3. **Braggers of themselves**. These people exalted themselves in word to appear better, but their bragging only revealed their insecurities.

4. **Flatters others for personal gain**. These people spend time with others in order to gain security for future needs. They *flatter* the rich hoping to gain what they need physically. The word means to show partiality for personal gain. These people could not be trusted with much responsibility because they only tried to gain attention to themselves by flattering others.

There will be false teachers who come in like stealth with a motive of feeding themselves rather than the church body. According to Scripture Christ is the Head of the church, but, He appoints under-shepherds to feed and teach the flock. Pastor Josh addressed the responsibility of shepherds in his sermon:

False teachers are liable to undermine the faith of others. They are shepherds that only look out for themselves. Shepherds are a common theme in the Bible. Ezekiel 34 is one of my favorite portions of Scripture because God Himself contrasts how an evil shepherd shepherds the flock with how He shepherds the flock.

Evil shepherds:

Thus says the Lord GOD to the shepherds: 'Woe to the shepherds of Israel who feed themselves! Should not the shepherds feed the flocks?
Ezekiel 34:2

> False teachers are liable to undermine the faith of others, they are shepherds that only look out for themselves.

Therefore, you shepherds, hear the word of the LORD: "As I live," says the Lord GOD, "surely because My flock became a prey, and My flock became food for every beast of the field, because there was no shepherd, nor did My shepherds search for My flock, but the shepherds fed themselves and did not feed My flock"—therefore, O shepherds, hear the word of the LORD! Thus says the Lord GOD: "Behold, I am against the shepherds, and I will require My flock at their hand; I will cause them to cease feeding the sheep, and the shepherds shall feed themselves no more; for I will deliver My flock from their mouths, that they may no longer be food for them."
Ezekiel 34:7-10

God as Shepherd:

I will make a covenant of peace with them, and cause wild beasts to cease from the land; and they will dwell safely in the wilderness and sleep in the woods. I will make them and the places all around My hill a blessing; and I will cause showers to come down in their season; there shall be showers of blessing. Then the trees of the field shall yield their fruit, and the earth shall yield her increase. They shall be safe in their land; and they shall know that I am the LORD, when I have broken the bands of their yoke and delivered them from the hand of those who enslaved them. And they shall no longer be a prey for the nations, nor shall beasts of the land devour them; but they shall dwell safely, and

no one shall make them afraid. I will raise up for them a garden of renown, and they shall no longer be consumed with hunger in the land, nor bear the shame of the Gentiles anymore. Thus they shall know that I, the LORD their God, am with them, and they, the house of Israel, are My people," says the Lord GOD. "You are My flock, the flock of My pasture; you are men, and I am your God," says the Lord GOD.
Ezekiel 34:25-31

God says, "This is how I shepherd the people in Israel: I know them, care for them, gather them together, bring them near, and give them peace. Don't you want peace? We live in such a broken world, but I want peace. I'm so grateful for God's Words in Ezekiel 34, where He says, "And I'll give them peace because I care for them. I'll gather them, and then I will not only be their Shepherd, but I will be their only Shepherd." The under-shepherd is to emulate the Messiah.

Shepherd the flock of God which is among you, serving as overseers, not by compulsion but willingly, not for dishonest gain but eagerly; nor as being lords over those entrusted to you, but being examples to the flock; and when the Chief Shepherd appears, you will receive the crown of glory that does not fade away.
1 Peter 5:2-4

Do you see the contrast that Scripture makes between shepherds? The evil shepherds were after themselves. At Flat Creek, we want to be good shepherds that emulate the Father."

Recognizing grumblers, complainers, and those who shepherd for selfish gain are all part of the responsibility of the church directed by the Head, Jesus. While a horse may rush into battle, many times the battle rushes into the church. The correct posture of the church is complete obedience to Jesus, which includes discerning spiritual battles involving evil spirits. This requires calling "*the holy day of the LORD honorable, and...not doing your own ways...*

Those who choose to go their own way cannot be considered godly regardless of how mild their actions may seem to others. The church cannot judge based upon human thinking. It must allow the Lord to judge those going their own way. The book of Jude discussed,

> *Now Enoch, the seventh from Adam, prophesied about these men also, saying, "Behold, the Lord comes with ten thousands of His saints, to execute judgment on all, to convict all who are ungodly among them of all their ungodly deeds which they have committed in an ungodly way, and of all the harsh things which ungodly sinners have spoken against Him."*
>
> **Jude 1:14-15**

Pastor Josh stated:

> *If you look at verse 4 of Jude, you will see that their judgment was predicted long ago. Those who come in with stealth, were ungodly, had turned the grace of the Lord into lewdness, and denied the only master and Lord Jesus Christ. The word* ungodly *is used four times in Jude 15. The purpose of the prediction was to let the saints know that God will execute judgment and convict the ungodly concerning all the harsh things they say about Jesus. They are those who live without reverence and repentance before God and walk ungodly performing evil deeds, thinking in ungodly ways, and using harsh and arrogant words concerning God. They complain without shame and use swollen words and flatter to take advantage. The Hebrew children are an illustration for us. They fought with God. They were critical. They were negative. Their source of thinking was their own evil desires. What is your source of thinking? They had a mind-set that said, "If it feels good, do it." They allowed their flesh to rule their lives. A lot of times we don't think about spiritual warfare that occurs through critical words. Yesterday, I was having a conversation about this very thing. I was discussing that Ephesians 4 tells us that we're to build up the saints. That we are one body, and that we are to encourage and edify one another.*
>
> *Spiritual warfare can manifest itself through critical words that tear down. I want us to be a church family where*

it is common nature to build up. I don't want critical, harsh spirits in this church that tear others down because that brings a spiritual warfare element.

In verse 14, Jude said the Lord comes with ten thousands of his holy saints. There is coming a day when Jesus will return, not just at the rapture, but to set up shop and to rule and reign forever. When He comes next, He is coming with a crown. He will not be heading to a cross. He is coming to a throne, not to a cradle. He will rule and reign, and He will not die because He is King of kings and Lord of lords. He will come to execute judgment. Matthew 10:28 says, "And do not fear those who kill the body but cannot kill the soul. But rather fear Him who is able to destroy both soul and body in hell." Spiritual warfare is no joke. What we're dealing with today is not a laughing matter. And I humbly suggest to you that if you've never made your heart right with God, today you can acknowledge this. I really believe God woke me up to tell you that He is a kind, loving, Heavenly Father and that by His kindness He leads us to repentance. But He is also holy, and He won't allow sin in His Presence. And so He gives you an opportunity now to respond to his grace and kindness. Will you respond?

The book of Jude speaks to the judgment of the ungodly, and Pastor Josh's sermon helps to reveal the gravity of what will happen to those who dishonor the name of Jesus. It is also important to remember God's correction to the Israelites in Isaiah 58. They used God's Ways for selfish gain. This was deceit and perversion. God corrected the Israelites by showing them the condition of their hearts. God's Way is based upon the condition of the heart. He not only wanted them to observe His holy day but also to not go their own way. It is not hard to recognize ungodly acts and ways, but it is hard to recognize those who are going God's Way for selfish gain. In fact, without discernment and wisdom from the Lord, you will probably consider those people godly.

Much like the horse is an extension of the rider through connection, the church is an extension of Christ through connection. Biblically the church is the body of Christ. When the body is not connected to the

Head, the church will not look like Jesus. Consider what it would look like for each member of the body to have their own personal walk with God and come together in unity. It would be a perfect picture of Jesus.

It is critical for the church to return to its purpose to imitate, love, and obey Jesus, the Head. The posture of the church should be to do whatever the Head tells it to do and not what people tell it to do.

The Body of Christ

Pastor Josh referenced Ephesians 4 in the previous section of the book regarding edifying and the building up of the saints. Around the time I was writing on this, Kerry and I were discussing the body of Christ. From that conversation he sent me some audio on his teachings from the book of Ephesians and quickly I remembered pastor Josh referencing it and knew it would be a perfect fit for this section of the book. Kerry has taught Ephesians 4 in a few churches over the years and has always hoped that it would be used in a book. There is a lesson to learn from this connection. Remember that if God is working in your life right now and you cannot see how any of what He is doing will be used, just remember that the timing is up to Him. God's timing to use what He began through Kerry's teaching on the book of Ephesians is now and is in line with pastor Josh's preaching of Jude as well as God's correction of the Israelites. This is very important because it demonstrates the body working together by allowing the Head, Jesus, to guide every decision made. Only God can guide Kerry to teach on Ephesians many years ago, and then connect it to what He guided pastor Josh to preach on many years later, in order to organize it in such a way that will help you to learn the value of each member of the body of Christ.

If we are going to understand how to train the church in love, we must first understand the structure of the body of Christ according to Scripture and not other people or organizations. To do that we will use excerpts from Kerry's teaching on Ephesians 4.

Let's start by breaking down each verse and then sharing Kerry's teaching.

> *But to each one of us grace was given according to the measure of Christ's gift.*
> **Ephesians 4:7**

Christ himself gives the gifts necessary to function properly as a New Testament church. In verse 11, we begin to see these gifts.

> *And He Himself gave some to be apostles, some prophets, some evangelists, and some pastors and teachers,*
> **Ephesians 4:11**

Every person who has been truly born-again has a gift from Christ. There is nothing you can do in and of yourself to earn it or achieve it. It is simply a grace gift from the Head of the church, Christ, to a member of the body or through a member of the body. In fact, the gift is not given to individuals but is given to the body. When you have a spiritual gift, you don't have the prerogative to use it any way you want. It wasn't given for you. It was given to build up the body.

Paul also discussed spiritual gifts in 1 Corinthians 12 but focused on the diversity of gifts. In this passage in Ephesians, he does not get into the diversity of the gifts such as: healing, mercy, or helps. The gifts discussed here in Ephesians come primarily in the picture of offices and not individual gifts to the body. These offices help the church to form a structure in order to function properly as Christ's body.

He starts with the office of apostle. Biblically there are two qualifications to be an apostle. First, one must be an eyewitness of the public ministry of Jesus. Second, one must have had a direct commission from Christ. These qualifications limit many from being an apostle. The function of an apostle is to only speak of infallible testimonies. For a testimony to be infallible, it must be God-oriented. This means that it doesn't come from people, but from God.

Chapter 4: Honor through Submission

The next office that Paul discussed was a prophet. A prophet is gifted to speak what the Lord tells him to speak. In the Old Testament, prophets corrected moral wrongs as directed by the Lord. A prophet's office function was to share the message that was provided by God.

Next, Paul discussed evangelists. Evangelists were those who founded churches. They would go out, usually on commission under the leadership of an apostle, and share what Jesus had done. An evangelist's function was to share what Christ has already accomplished for the person through salvation.

The last office Paul discussed was the pastor/teacher. In some older translations, you will see "pastor, teacher" as though it is two positions. In the New King James translation, you see *pastor and teacher*. In the original language, if you look at this office you will find, pastor-teacher. This is one office with two functions. A pastor's responsibility was to rule and guide as a bishop. In our day, we don't use the term *bishop* in many churches, but understand the role biblically of a pastor as a ruling elder who guides as that of a shepherd guiding the flock. The teacher side of that responsibility is to build up and teach the church how to function in faith.

These offices are a blessing to the church as a gift from Christ. The gift is not only the office but also the person who Christ assigns to these offices. The church is established as Christ being the Head. However, the pastor is the one who guides the flock. He's not the head but he serves under the Headship of Christ to lead and guide that church. The sole purpose of these gifts are to provide spiritual growth to the body.

That is why some are proclaiming the Word of God, some are evangelizing, and some are establishing a foundation for a local church. There is also the pastor-teacher who is guiding, ruling, and teaching them in the body. Each office has a unique function but all offices lead to one purpose:

> The teacher side of that responsibility is to build up and teach the church how to function in faith... The purpose of these gifts are to provide spiritual growth to the body.

for the equipping of the saints for the work of ministry, for the edifying of the body of Christ,
Ephesians 4:12

Christ provided these gifts for the equipping of the saints, for the work of the ministry, and for the edification of the body of Christ. Many times people think the pastor and staff of the church are the only ones who are supposed to do all the work of the ministry. In the original languages, it is clear that the job of these offices is to equip the saints to do the work of the ministry.

Kerry's role when he was senior associate pastor and Pastor Josh's role as senior pastor was and is to equip the saints to do the work of the ministry. While they will also do work in the ministry, their main function is to equip others to serve.

Kerry recalled receiving a phone call while serving a church. *I answered the phone and the person on the other line said, "Kerry, some new people moved in down the street from us and I thought you needed to go visit them and ask them to come to our church."*

I responded, "I would be glad to go and visit them. When would you like to go?"

God brought that person across this person's path and not mine. My job is to equip the person to do the work of the ministry.

The equipping of the saints is to build up the body of Christ "till we all come to the unity of the faith and of the knowledge of the Son of God, to a perfect man, to the measure of the stature of the fullness of Christ" (Ephesians 4:13). It is important to have an understanding of the goal of equipping and building of the body because it is the purpose of the church. As members are built up, they begin to look more and more like Christ, providing unity within the church. The church is not built up into the Head if there is no unity. Because to be built up in Christ is to have the same motive and purpose for ministry, to help build others up into Christ by teaching them how to have a relationship with Jesus. This provides protection from straying off course.

> It is important to have an understanding of the goal of equipping and building of the body because it is the purpose of the church.

Chapter 4: Honor through Submission

> *that we should no longer be children, tossed to and fro and carried about with every wind of doctrine, by the trickery of men, in the cunning craftiness of deceitful plotting,*
> **Ephesians 4:14**

Paul knew there were people in the churches acting like children. You help children by treating them like children. Paul wanted the people to move past acting like children so he could teach them deeper things. So he said, don't be children tossed to and fro and carried about by every wind of doctrine. Notice that Paul didn't say don't be tossed to and fro by every *false* doctrine. He said every wind of doctrine. If someone in the body of Christ only ever discusses one truth, that person will be blown off course, unless it's the foundation of the gospel.

Have you ever shared Jesus with someone only to have that person change the subject? This recently happened to Alison. She was on a cruise and was sitting alone having her quiet time with her Bible open. A man came to her and started asking random questions he had about the Bible. He began with, "Do you think a body should be buried or cremated?

Then he said, "You mean to tell me a man can murder someone and another man can steal and they are both going to hell unless they confess?"

"I do not have all the answers, but I know that you must believe in Jesus Christ. The key is Jesus," Alison responded.

After that response the man said, "Ok, I will leave you alone now."

> **The key is Jesus.**

Alison began to pray and ask God whether or not this was someone He wanted her to talk to or just a distraction to keep her from spending time with Him. Right after she finished praying the man came back.

He asked, "You mean to tell me Baptists can't drink?"

Again Alison replied, "I am telling you it is about believing on Jesus and loving God."

He was not interested in any conversation about Jesus. This told Alison that it was a distraction. She did not engage in discussing the questions that he kept asking but rather stayed focused on Jesus. The way someone responds when you discuss Jesus reveals the condition of his heart as well as his motive.

> *but, speaking the truth in love, may grow up in all things into Him who is the head—Christ—from whom the whole body, joined and knit together by what every joint supplies, according to the effective working by which every part does its share, causes growth of the body for the edifying of itself in love.*
> **Ephesians 4:15-16**

This is a great example of fixating on one topic of the Bible. This can lead to arguments rather than edification. It is important to walk away from those conversations so that you are not distracted from what really matters. The minute you engage in an argument over doctrine you are not speaking the truth in love.

> *The minute you engage in an argument over doctrine you are not speaking the truth in love.*

Love is a fruit of the Spirit of God and is the motive of a Christian walking in the Spirit. Building up a person into the Head means teaching them how to walk in the Spirit of Christ. The motive of any argument is to win, not to build up another person in Christ. Saying that you are speaking the truth in love is not the same as actually speaking the truth in love. Love's motive is not to be right, make the person agree with you, or win an argument. Those are all the motives of the flesh. The motive of love is to edify and build up the body into the Head–Jesus. Most people only want to get their own way and will use Scripture to do so if necessary.

The whole body must be at work. No one in the body can sin without affecting the entire body. Scripture doesn't say that a church isn't growing because it doesn't have the right pastor or the right staff or the right deacons. However, Scripture does teach that if a body is not effectively working together, there will be no growth. Every member of the body is critical in playing an active role in growing the church into the Head. Church members are just as important to the church as any of the offices Jesus gave the church. It is important to remember what you are a member of when thinking on this truth.

> *For we are members of His body, of His flesh and of His bones.*
> **Ephesians 5:30**

Chapter 4: Honor through Submission

Biblically to be a member of the church is to be a member of Christ's body, flesh, and bones. Consider your physical body for a moment. In order for each part to function properly your brain sends messages to each part individually. For example, your arm does not move unless your brain tells it to. If your arm moved on its own, then your body would be in trouble. It is an unhealthy body that moves independently from the brain. This is the same concept regarding Christ's Body. There are many members who are not connected to the Head, but are instead connected to the pastor or other members. Because of this, it is critical for the saints who are connected to Jesus to continue to grow in order to help the weaker members grow as well.

If the body disconnects from the Head, then it will die spiritually. Churches are dying now because they have stopped listening to Jesus.

And He is the head of the body, the church, who is the beginning, the firstborn from the dead, that in all things He may have the preeminence.

Colossians 1:18

Christ is the beginning of the Church just as He is the beginning of creation. The Church did not come into existence before Christ became the Head. Rather, Christ birthed the Church. The Head gives direction and life to the Church. Without Him the Church would not have life. Just as life flows from the Vine into the branches (see John 15), life also flows from the Head to the body. As He flows into the body, unity is developed among those who receive and follow Him. He is the firstborn of the dead. The Church received life as Christ was raised from the dead. Christ must have preeminence in everything. He created all of the universe, the Church, and life itself. He must increase, and we must decrease.

> Christ is the beginning of the Church just as He is the beginning of creation.

Honor through Submission

Webster's dictionary defines *honor* as, "esteem due or paid to worth; high estimation, respect, consideration, and reverence." The dictionary lists a few more definitions involving the idea of fame, and recognition.

As a believer your life is to honor the only One Who is worthy of honor and praise–Jesus. Honor represents esteem but in this case it is not self-esteem. To honor the Lord is to live the life you were called by God to live.

> **To honor the Lord is to live the life you were called by God to live.**

Now to the King eternal, immortal, invisible, to God who alone is wise, be honor and glory forever and ever. Amen.
1 Timothy 1:17

Worthy is the Lamb who was slain to receive power and riches and wisdom, and strength and honor and glory and blessing!
Revelation 5:12

In order for the church to honor the Lord and call His day honorable, it must submit to God. According to Isaiah 58:13, God desires you to honor Him by not going your own way. In this verse He tells you what to do, *call the Holy day of the Lord honorable*, and then He tells you what not to do, *not doing [or going] your own ways*. Pastor Josh's sermon on Jude illustrates the ungodly and evil ways that were taking place in different stories in the Bible, such as the way of Cain, the error of Balaam, and the rebellion of Korah. When reading these it is not hard to recognize their evil ways. However, sometimes an evil way can be more subtle in your own life. God will never ask you to sin in order to go His Way.

> **God will never ask you to sin in order to go His Way.**

Sometimes people are confused about what it means to go God's Way. While there are some commands that the average believer knows should obviously be avoided, there are also daily commands that God has for you and the church in order to build a relationship with Him. These commands are for everyday decisions. You go your own way when you make decisions for personal gain. This honors self instead of Jesus and harms the whole church.

Jehoshaphat was the king of Judah. The Lord was with Jehoshaphat because Jehoshaphat walked in the ways of the Lord. He did not walk according to the sins of Israel but worshipped God instead of idols. Because of this God established the kingdom in his hand and gave him riches and honor in abundance. His heart delighted in the Lord's ways so much so that he removed the high places from Judah. When there came a warning to Ahab, king of Israel, who Jehoshaphat was allied to, Jehoshaphat sought the Word of the Lord. He entered battle alongside Ahab, and returned home in peace even though Ahab died. (see 2 Chronicles 17-19).

Some time later Jehoshaphat entered another battle. Judah gathered together to ask the Lord for help. Jehoshaphat prayed in the assembly of Judah and Jerusalem saying,

> *"O Lord God of our fathers, are You not God in heaven, and do You not rule over all the kingdoms of the nations, and in Your hand is there not power and might, so that no one is able to withstand You? Are You not our God, who drove out the inhabitants of this land before Your people Israel, and gave it to the descendants of Abraham Your friend forever? And they dwell in it, and have built You a sanctuary in it for Your name, saying, "If disaster comes upon us–sword, judgment, pestilence, or famine–we will stand before this temple and in Your presence (for Your name is in this temple), and cry out to You in our affliction, and You will hear and save.' And now, here are the people of Ammon, Moab, and Mount Seir–whom You would not let Israel invade when they came out of the land of Egypt, but they turned from them and did not destroy them–here they are, rewarding us by coming to throw us out of Your possession which You have given us to inherit. O our God, will You not judge them? For we have no power against this great multitude that is coming against us; nor do we know what to do, but our eyes are upon You." (2 Chronicles 20:5-12).*

The Lord responded through the Spirit saying,

> *And he said, "Listen, all you of Judah and you inhabitants of Jerusalem, and you, King Jehoshaphat! Thus says the LORD to you: 'Do not be afraid nor dismayed because*

of this great multitude, for the battle is not yours, but God's. Tomorrow go down against them. They will surely come up by the Ascent of Ziz, and you will find them at the end of the brook before the Wilderness of Jeruel. You will not need to fight in this battle. Position yourselves, stand still and see the salvation of the LORD, who is with you, O Judah and Jerusalem!' Do not fear or be dismayed; tomorrow go out against them, for the LORD is with you" (2 Chronicles 20:15-17).

> **Jehoshaphat obeyed God and through singing and praise the Lord defeated his enemies.**

Jehoshaphat obeyed God, and through singing and praise the Lord defeated his enemies.

Because Jehoshaphat honored God, God honored Jehoshaphat and through this honor he in turn was honored as well. He delighted in God, which is what God called the Israelites to do in Isaiah 58. This teaches us that we can know God's Will in every situation if we seek Him. This is a great example of how the church today needs to honor the Lord. God's Way for Jehoshaphat was to stand still and praise the Lord. What would the human way be in this situation? It would not have been to stand still. Many times the church may seek the Lord, hear from the Lord, and then twist His response to fit the way it wants to go. This is what God wanted the Israelites to change in order to honor Him.

The Word of the Lord to Saul was much different than the Word that He gave to Jehoshaphat. The Lord sent Samuel to deliver His message to Saul. Samuel said to Saul,

> *"The LORD sent me to anoint you king over His people, over Israel. Now therefore, heed the voice of the words of the LORD. Thus says the LORD of hosts: "I will punish Amalek for what he did to Israel, how he ambushed him on the way when he came up from Egypt. Now go and attack Amalek, and utterly destroy all that they have, and do not spare them. But kill both man and woman, infant and nursing child, ox and sheep, camel and donkey'."*
>
> **1 Samuel 15:1-3**

While God asked Jehoshaphat to praise Him and stand still, He commanded Saul to destroy everything. Many times Christians will use a message they received from God in the past to help them in a situation they are facing today. This is not honoring God because you do not know if that is the message that He has for that particular situation. Think about it this way. If Saul knew the Word that God spoke to Jehoshaphat for his battle, Saul may have assumed that he was to stand still in his battle. All believers lean on what God told them in past situations when they are not up to date in their relationship with God. This is dangerous when God wants to do something different in the new situation.

Unlike Jehoshaphat, Saul did not obey God's command.

> *"But Saul and the people spared Agag and the best of the sheep, the oxen, the fatlings, the lambs, and all that was good, and were unwilling to utterly destroy them. But everything despised and worthless, that they utterly destroyed."*
> **1 Samuel 15:9**

Saul and the people kept what they thought was the best even though God said to destroy everything. In God's eyes, the best of evil is still evil. This is why you cannot lean on your own thinking and claim to follow God. God told Samuel that He regretted placing Saul as king. When Samuel went to tell Saul what God told him, Saul responded that he performed the commandment of God.

> **In God's eyes, the best of evil is still evil.**

> *"Then Samuel said to Saul, "Be quiet! And I will tell you what the LORD said to me last night." And he said to him, "Speak on." So Samuel said, "When you were little in your own eyes, were you not head of the tribes of Israel? And did not the LORD anoint you king over Israel? Now the LORD sent you on a mission, and said, "Go, and utterly destroy the sinners, the Amalekites, and fight against them until they are consumed.' Why then did you not obey the voice of the LORD? Why did you swoop down on the spoil, and do evil in the sight of the LORD?" And Saul said to Samuel, "But I have obeyed the voice of the LORD, and gone on the mission on which the LORD sent me, and brought back Agag king of Amalek; I have utterly destroyed the Amalekites."*
> **1 Samuel 15:16-20**

Saul obeyed some of God's command, but did not destroy everything God told him to. In his prideful mind, Saul thought he obeyed because he accomplished some of the command. When confronted, he blamed the people. This is typical of the flesh. Samuel told Saul that when he was little in his own eyes he was head of the tribe. But now he had gone his own way. Pride can make you believe you are following God, because you are deceived into thinking that you are god. This thinking does not honor the Lord. It is a dangerous place to be. Saul placed himself and all the people under him in a dangerous position because he did not obey.

> Pride can make you believe you are following God because you are deceived into thinking that you are god.

God asked the Israelites to honor Him by not going their own way. This is a call to repentance. It is a call to submission to God. When a horse's mind is not under submission to its rider, it is dangerous for the rider. However, the horse may obey the rider in some areas even when the horse is not submitted to the rider. But the horse will only obey as long as he is not distracted. Submission to God is not only in word or action but also in thought and desire. You will know if you honor God through submission when He brings a situation across your path in which you do not agree. The way in which you handle the situation will reveal where your heart and mind are focused. When you do not honor God through submission as a believer, you are hurting His entire body.

Riding on High Hills Devotion Chapter 4

Honor through Submission

"The holy day of the LORD honorable, and shall honor Him, not doing your own ways..."
Isaiah 58:13

In order to train the church in love, you need to submit to God. Much like training a horse, discipleship involves several personalities and levels of growth. If you don't submit to God, you will not be able to reach those who are not like you and will end up with a body of believers that have your selfish desires. When you honor God by not going your own way, He will develop the church based on His desires and bring people to help you in the areas you struggle with.

Anything created by God deserves honor including His holy day. The Israelites took what God designed and used it for their own gain. They had no desire to go God's Way and had lost sight of the purpose of the Lord's Day. One way that God reveals wrongdoing is through discipline. In Isaiah 58:13, He provided instruction on how to return to His Ways. Discipline leads you back into the Ways of God and allows you to experience the power and majesty of the Lord. It is a complete lie to believe that God will not discipline those He loves. If you believe your way is better than God's Way, you will have a very low view of God and a high view of self.

> Discipline is designed to lead you back into the Ways of God and allows you to experience the power and majesty of the Lord.

How prideful can a person be to believe that they can come up against God and win? It is this same pride that drives a person to believe they can overpower a horse. In order to honor a horse, you must humble yourself and recognize that you cannot overpower it physically. By continuing to go your own way as a believer, you are not honoring the Lord. Think about the message that it sends to God when you take His design and pervert it in order to get your own way. This is not only dishonoring but also hurtful. Honor requires more than just words; it also requires submission. If you are unwilling to submit your way to God, then you are not honoring Him.

> Honor requires more than just words, it requires submission.

Submission is an unpopular concept because it is misunderstood. When a horse is willing to submit to you, both you and the horse enjoy the time together. But when the horse resists, you are both miserable. To honor God through submission provides love, joy, and peace that is beyond human comprehension which is a much better way to live. God desires you to go His Way, because He knows that sin will only provide misery and struggle. Honor the Lord today by submitting to His Way.

The Church's Posture #4
God desires to patiently teach you the way of the Spirit in order for you to live in fellowship with Him. You will not accomplish this without submitting your way to the Lord.

Honor The Horse: Riding Principle #4
Honor the horse by learning its way and patiently teaching it your way.

Chapter 4: Honor through Submission

Chapter 5: Surrendering Your Way

RIDING PRINCIPLE #5

RESPECT THE HORSE

A horse tends to obey until you ask it to do something it does not want to do. It is important while training a horse to recognize your limits and respect the power and strength of the animal. There is a difference between a horse not understanding what you are asking and disobeying you. There will come a time when the horse will resist. If the horse is resisting and you continue to allow this behavior without any correction, you may find yourself in a dangerous situation.

The horse needs to respect you. A horse that is disrespectful can hurt you. The way to train a horse to respect your space is to teach it boundaries. The horse should expect work when it disobeys and rest when it obeys. When you train in this way, you establish the horse's respect in your relationship. Before you decide that the horse is disobeying, you should make sure the horse in not in pain. For example, if a horse acts up when you put on the girth, the horse could be disobeying or be in pain. Check the area by rubbing it to see if the same reaction happens. Once you rule out pain you can accept that it is disobedience and move on to correction.

> The horse should expect work when it disobeys and rest when it obeys.

A horse will test boundaries. If the horse gets away with disobedience, then it will begin testing you in other areas. This creates a relationship that is unenjoyable. Consistency is the key in establishing a respectful relationship. When dealing with a horse that is testing you, consider whether or not you are afraid of the horse. Fear and training is not a good combination. If you allow the horse to disobey your boundaries, then you will lose control, and the horse will continue pushing you around. There may come a time when you need a professional trainer to correct an issue with your horse. The trainer can teach you how to move forward without fear. As you gain confidence

> Consistency is the key in establishing a respectful relationship.

and learn how far your horse will push you, you will no longer be afraid. As long as you do not know what you are doing and the purpose of it, you will not have confidence. Boundaries are hard for so many people because people see boundaries as unloving. That could not be further from the truth. Healthy relationships cannot exist without healthy boundaries.

> Healthy relationships cannot exist without healthy boundaries.

Chapter 5
Surrendering Your Way

"... Nor finding your own pleasure, nor speaking your own words,..."
Isaiah 58:13

A common theme often surfaces when teaching people about horse safety. Things such as where to stand, how to walk around the horse, and how to hold the lead rope are a few of those lessons. Many people have no fear of this large animal until you begin discussing safety procedures. This is intriguing. Knowledge demands respect. Once you know something, you are then responsible for that knowledge. It is a positive thing to have a healthy fear of a horse. A cautious smart fear provides protection to the rider.

> **Knowledge demands respect.**

He does not delight in the strength of the horse; He takes no pleasure in the legs of a man. The LORD takes pleasure in those who fear Him, in those who hope in His mercy.
Psalm 147:10-11

Healthy fear is equal to reverence or respect and is the requirement to please the Lord. Without respect for the horse's power and strength, you can become injured. The same holds true with God. When you refuse to surrender your way, you communicate

> **By learning Truth, you learn boundary lines.**

with God that you do not respect Him and His Way. By learning Truth, you learn boundary lines. Your training must begin where your heart does not line up with God's boundaries. Every time a lead rope, bridle, saddle, or any other piece of equipment is applied to a horse, you are asking the horse to surrender his way.

The concept of healthy boundaries is seemingly lost in the church. This is confusing considering that the entirety of the Bible consists of boundaries for the believer provided by God to keep you in the love of Christ. Without boundaries you would continue to go your own way, find your own pleasure, and speak your own words. Healthy boundaries are necessary with horses because of their strength and size. They do not have to do what you are asking them to do. They can easily overpower you. Instead, many submit to the direction of the rider. This is truly amazing.

Until the church gains healthy boundaries in relationship to Jesus, the body risks finding their own pleasure and speaking their own words. Pastor Josh prayed at the beginning of his sermon, "God, I beg of You today that I don't say anything stupid but that I would be faithful to your text. Thank You for being my Defender. Thank You for being our Defender, and thank You for rising from the grave. This is Your church, and the gates of hell will not prevail against it."

> Until the church gains healthy boundaries in relationship to Jesus, the body risks finding their own pleasure and speaking their own words.

Respect Through Boundaries

Blessed is that man who makes the LORD his trust, and does not respect the proud, nor such as turn aside to lies.

Psalm 40:4

Respect tends to be a concept that everyone demands but few offer in return. It seems there is some confusion in regard to respect. Many times Christians confuse salvation with other character-earned qualities. Salvation is not earned but gifted to those who believe on Jesus Christ. You cannot perform enough good deeds to earn salvation because God only grants it to a person who truly believes. However, this is not true for all aspects of character-earned blessings. Respect is one of those blessings.

Respect is earned and given to those who humble themselves and live for Christ. According to Psalm 40:4 you should not respect the proud. This reveals that there are boundaries regarding the concept of who is to be respected and who is not to be respected. A Christian should care about the boundaries that come from God, not the world. The world respects the powerful, wealthy, and proud. God respects those who submit their lives to Him in humility and live according to His Ways.

> Respect is earned and given to those who humble themselves and live for Christ.

Jude wanted to write about salvation but found it necessary to write about contending for the faith. How can you contend for the faith without boundaries and respect? It is impossible to contend for the faith without establishing what you are for and what you are against. It is important to note here that it is possible to love someone while not respecting their ways. Many lump love and respect together while not understanding the concept of God's Love.

To respect sin is to disrespect God. If someone in the church is causing division or living in sin, the church needs to correct this person in love. This means allowing the Spirit to correct. When those in the body of Christ are not walking in the Spirit, they are not qualified to make corrections. The flesh cannot properly correct in love. Jude urged those who are called, sanctified, and preserved to contend for the faith. *Contend* means to wrestle, fight, and battle for the faith that "was once for all delivered to the saints." The key is that "we do not wrestle against flesh and blood" (Ephesians 6:12).

> The flesh cannot properly correct in love.

Kerry teaches, "We are here to fight for the kingdom of heaven and against the enemies of heaven. In Christ, you have the ability to stand against the devil. Christ living in you gives you power to stand against the attacks of the evil one. If you are not well-grounded biblically, and if you do not have a good, solid walk with Christ day by day, then you will follow the wrong voice. If you are walking in a strong, intimate, daily relationship with Christ, you will hear His voice when He speaks and it will protect you from the voice of the enemy."

My sheep hear My voice, and I know them, and they follow Me. And I give them eternal life, and they shall never perish; neither shall anyone snatch them out of My hand.
John 10:27-28

Jude warned the saints that ungodly men had crept into the church and turned God's grace into lewdness. Those who do not hear the voice of Christ will follow these type of men. These men disrespected the grace of God and followed the ways of the enemy, the ways of sin. While you are not to respect the devil and his ways, you must respect the fact that the devil is more cunning and powerful than you, but he is not more powerful than Christ. The church is in trouble because the enemy has found a weakness in the body: people who are not walking with God. When leaders in the body of Christ do not walk in the Spirit, the church is wide open for the wiles of the enemy.

> When leaders in the body of Christ do not walk in the Spirit, it leaves the church wide open for the wiles of the enemy.

Pastor Josh preached,

Jude is talked about putting all of yourself into this fight for the faith that was delivered to the saints. Some acted like they were friendly and came into the church. They gained a following. That did not happen overnight. It came through stealth. And here, Jude is saying, you should fight and contend for the faith. The problem is that many of us are scared to fight. We just need to understand that God has called us to fight spiritually.

We contend. We fight. We wrestle. We have a grid-iron faith every day. Every day for our family, for our marriage, for our children, for our own soul, we step up and say, "Lord, here am I. Send me to contend, to fight." Why? Because there are some who are stealthy. There are some who you think are friendly, but Jude reminded us they are ungodly. He didn't leave us to wonder why. They have taken God's amazing grace and have twisted it into a license to sin. They say, "I can cohabit with my other friend because I have grace. I can expose myself to all sorts of drugs because

I have grace. I can live an immoral lifestyle," which Jude dealt with directly, *because I have grace, and they use grace as a license for a behavior that is contrary to the Will of God. God opposes every bit of it and does not put His hand of favor on it.*

God has a boundary regarding His grace: "God resists the proud, but gives grace to the humble" (James 4:6). Grace does not provide a license to sin. When anyone lives as though it does, they are disrespecting God. The truth is that it is far better to contend for the faith than to contend against God. When you wrestle against God, you never win. Seeking your own pleasure and claiming that God's grace accepts it is highly disrespectful and will also disqualify you from wrestling for the faith. Do you desire to lead God's church astray? God said in Isaiah 58 to stop finding your own pleasure and speaking your own words. If you desire to respect God, then you must stay within His boundary lines.

> Grace does not provide a license to sin.

If the body of Christ is to contend for the faith, then the church must train members to stay within the love of Christ instead of training them to stay in relationship with prideful people who follow deception. It is true that reconciliation is always the goal. But truth cannot reconcile with deception. Staying in the love of Christ will not be accomplished by saying things like "We all belong," or "Everyone is welcome." This is not biblical. There are requirements to be in the family of God. The greatest requirement for a born-again believer is to follow God's Way and not his own way. If you do not believe that is so, then you do not believe the main truths of the book of Isaiah. You will not ride on high hills and experience the heritage of Jacob as long as you continue to go your own way, seek your own pleasure, and speak your own words.

The horse deserves respect because God created it and the unique aspects that make up the horse. This is the same for the church. The church deserves respect because God established it. It is not respectful to blur the

> The church deserves respect because God established it.

boundary lines of God. God's boundaries are set up out of love for your protection. In order for you to not be caught in the trap of the enemy you must stay in fellowship with Jesus. God's boundaries keep you in the love of Christ and in His fellowship. The boundaries of God begin with a call to a relationship, continue through growth in sanctification, and finally preserve you until the day you leave this earth to be with Him in eternity.

The Called, The Sanctified, The Preserved (Kept)

Jude wrote "to those who are called, sanctified by God the Father, and preserved in Jesus Christ" (Jude 1:1). Pastor Josh preached, "Jude did not write to a pastor, a local assembly of pastors, or a convention or a denomination. He wrote to those who were called, loved, and kept for Jesus Christ."

The Lord called Kerry and Josh to vocational ministry and Alison to Biblical counseling. A calling is much different than a job because it is from the Lord. A calling is a strong burden and desire from God that is almost impossible to walk away from. Pastor Josh shared about the night God called him to the ministry:

I was 16 years old and was at a student camp. Dr. David Adams was preaching. I can't remember a lot about what he said, but two things are vivid in my mind and in my heart. The first thing that I remember is that God tapped me on the shoulder and spoke to my heart, "I am calling you into vocational ministry." I remember two specific calls:

1. To give myself continuously to prayer and the ministry of the Word.
2. To serve any of the saints whom He calls me to serve.

That night the Holy Spirit of God put a weight in my soul, and a burden in my heart. I left that place knowing that I had a purpose and a mission in life. I have not looked back since that night.

Just like Josh, Kerry was called to the ministry when he was a teenager.

> *When I was an older teenager, God began to deal with me about surrendering my whole life to Him and serving in the Gospel ministry. I had never desired the life of a pastor and was making other plans for my life. As on the day of my salvation, I could not resist the work of the Holy Spirit. It was at that time that I committed my life to the work of the ministry. This was a new beginning for me. I had planned to get married, have a nice family, and work a "regular" job. But that was not God's plan.*

Alison's call to biblical counseling happened in her late twenties at the time of her salvation.

> *God saved me from two house fires in my teenage years. At the time of my salvation, it was clear to me that I should not be alive and that He saved me for a purpose. I decided to surrender my whole life to Him and knew He wanted me to be a counselor. At the time, I did not know what that entailed but I did know that God desired to bring His counsel back to His church.*

While all three authors have a slightly different story regarding God calling them into ministry, there are a few similarities to consider. The first call that God places on the lives of His children is a call to a relationship. He desires to know you and reveal Himself to you in a personal way. Everything else flows out of that relationship. When God calls you into ministry, you must surrender your whole life. You can no longer live according to your pleasures and ways. When the Holy Spirit lays a calling on your life, you will never forget it. That moment will be etched into your mind forever. During times of struggle the Holy Spirit will bring to your remembrance that moment to keep you in pursuit of the call through a relationship with Christ.

The term *sanctified* means to be made holy. As a child of God, you should find yourself growing in what the Bible calls the sanctification process. Jesus prayed for His disciples, "Sanctify them by Your truth. Your word is truth" (John 17:17). Jude wrote not only to the called, but also to the sanctified, those growing in Christ. The longer you walk with the Lord, you should notice that you are not the same person as when you began the journey. You should recognize a completely different mind-set and desire for your life.

> *And such were some of you. But you were washed, but you were sanctified, but you were justified in the name of the Lord Jesus and by the Spirit of our God.*
> **1 Corinthians 6:11**

How can you contend for the faith if you are not being sanctified? Paul listed the unrighteous acts that would not inherit the Kingdom of God to the Corinthians. Then, he said, "And such were some of you. However, now you have been washed, sanctified, and justified." The truth is that anyone who continues to live in unrighteousness, claiming to love Christ, is deceived. When you live for sin, you will not care about the things of God, but will care about your own pleasures and your own words and ways even if you do outward acts that look godly.

> **How can you contend for the faith if you are not being sanctified?**

Jude's letter was to the called, sanctified, and preserved (see Jude 1:1). At the start of the letter there is a boundary. Jude prayed, "Mercy, peace, and love be multiplied" to those who were called, sanctified, and preserved. Scripture is a boundary line for those who love God and walk with Him. Alarmingly this realization reveals that a large number of Christians do not live with boundaries in their lives. In fact, they believe that by not setting boundaries they are doing the Lord's will. Yet, without boundaries you cannot be preserved and kept in the love of Christ.

> **Without boundaries you cannot be preserved and kept in the love of Christ.**

> *The LORD shall preserve you from all evil; He shall preserve your soul.*
> **Psalm 121:7**

Chapter 5: Surrendering Your Way

Whoever seeks to save his life will lose it, and whoever loses his life will preserve it.
Luke 17:33

Here is another boundary taught by Jesus: those who lose their lives will preserve them. If you are unwilling to surrender your life to Christ, then you are not preserved and kept in His Love. In each author's testimony, they share that they gave their lives to the calling. They laid down the lives they lived to that point and picked up the lives that Jesus provided. This is not only eternal life in heaven but also eternal life now. Living eternal life now requires boundaries. The Holy Spirit will teach you these boundary lines. It is crucial for the church that those who God calls to ministry step up and pursue the call. The body needs leaders who God placed in office, not those that put themselves in position.

> The body needs leaders who God placed in office, not those that put themselves in position.

Pastor Josh preached, "Unconditional love does not mean unconditional approval of one's behavior. I am begging you today not to put your hand on something that God is completely against. You can love the person, but do not back off of the truth of God's Word." If you desire to move on to the delight that God speaks about in Isaiah 58:14, then you must stay within the boundary lines of God's Word.

The Function of the Office

Just because someone is in an office ordained by God does not mean they are functioning properly. While we should have respect for the office as a gift from God, we do not need to obey someone in the office who is not functioning properly. This is true for the family as well. For example, you respect your parents because of their position but you do not need to surrender to them if they are sinning. This is also true of your pastor. However, you need discernment to determine if a pastor is functioning properly. Not all members of the body have a strong enough relationship with God to have discernment. This can result in following the pastor when he leads them astray.

The called, sanctified, and preserved (kept) must surrender their own pleasures and their own words. This means that any person in a church office is there as a representative of Christ and not a representative of self. It does not matter if that person believes that a certain program or event will be fun for the body. What matters is whether or not God will find it beneficial for the spiritual development of His people. If believers are not careful they will mimic the world in the church making the church unrecognizable. Unfortunately this is happening in many churches and families today.

> The function of each office requires the manifestation and gifting of the Holy Spirit.

The function of each office requires the empowerment of the Holy Spirit. While skills can be helpful, God does not call people based upon their skills. He calls them based upon their character. Therefore, the first responsibility of anyone in a church office is a love relationship with Jesus. When that is not in tact, the Holy Spirit will not flow freely through the person. Considering that Christ is the Head of the church, members of the church cannot know what to do without walking with Him daily. One does not need to be in an office to function in the body of Christ. Every assignment God gives is important. For the body to function properly "every part does its share" (Ephesians 4:16). If you do not do your part, you will hurt other parts of the body.

God assigned pastors and teachers "for the equipping of the saints for the work of ministry, for the edifying of the body of Christ" (Ephesians 4:12). The saints are built up into the Head by leadership and teaching, to do the work of the ministry that God assigns. If everyone does his part, the body will look like Jesus. Every part is important, and none is above the others. However, there are some positions that hold greater accountability. God does not take it lightly when a leader leads His children astray.

Your greatest responsibility as a believer is to walk with the Lord in a love relationship every single day and obey Him. If you keep your mind focused on that, then you will function properly no matter your assignment. But there are dangers along the way. There are many voices that want to tell the body what to do and there are "principalities, powers, rulers of the darkness of the age, and spiritual hosts of wickedness" that will attack, persecute, and try to stop the will of God at every corner (Ephesians 6:12). You must stay humble in knowing that the Holy Spirit is the only power that can go against the enemy.

Christianity is a battle not a party. The purpose of the church is to prepare the body to contend for the faith. The purpose of the family is to do the same. You cannot prepare for challenges by having fun. You must look at the parts of your heart that are vulnerable to the wiles of the enemy. When you allow God to clean those parts out of you by surrendering your way, seeking what pleases Him, and speaking His words, you leave the enemy with no place to trick you. The greatest point of temptation is your desires. When your desire is God's desire then temptations have no effect on you. It is not fun to look at the condition of your heart. However, if the body of Christ is going to function properly, it is the only way to get there.

> Christianity is a battle not a party.

Surrender Your Way

God's boundary lines in Isaiah 58:13 include "not doing your own ways, nor finding your own pleasures, nor speaking your own words." To honor the Lord's Day is to surrender your own way. It is also surrendering your own pleasures and speaking your own words. Webster's dictionary defines *pleasure* as "the gratification of the senses or of the mind; agreeable emotions; the excitement, relish or happiness produced by enjoyment or the expectation of good; opposed to pain." God is not interested in removing pleasure from your life, but in changing the object of your pleasure. In your sinful flesh, you find pleasure in sin. Sin is what nailed Jesus to the cross. He died to set you free from your sins. So when you find pleasure in your sin you are crossing the boundaries set by God. This means more than finding pleasure in sexual immorality, drugs, and other behavioral sins. This also means finding pleasure in making a name for yourself, building your own kingdom, and speaking your own words.

> God is not interested in removing pleasure from your life, but in changing the object of your pleasure.

When your heart is surrendered to God you will find pleasure in Him instead of sin. You will hunger and thirst for His Word and will desire to obey Him. You will experience freedom in your mind through peace and rest and will no longer desire living your life by going your own way.

God's people were perverting God's Ways in Isaiah 58:13-14. The leaders were using fasting as a means to get their own way with the people and then scolding God for not blessing their fasting. In Jeremiah, false prophets were speaking their own words and claiming they were God's Words (see Jeremiah 23:16-22). People today are doing the same things. God does not take this lightly because this will never profit His people. As long as you continue to find your own pleasure and speak your own words, you will not find joy in Christ. Joy comes to an obedient heart. If you desire to delight in the Lord, you must obey God's boundary to not find your own pleasure or speak your own words.

Chapter 5: Surrendering Your Way

Riding on High Hills Devotion Chapter 5

Surrendering Your Way

> *"... Nor finding your own pleasure, nor speaking your own words,..."*
>
> **Isaiah 58:13**

God's desire in Isaiah 58:13 is very clear. It is to the point and requires a response from His people. The response will either be obedience or disobedience. When training a person in discipleship, there must be clear communication and boundaries. This is also true for the horse.

It is one thing for a person or horse to not understand what is being asked of them and quite another for them to understand and continue going the wrong way. Many Christians are miserable and do not understand why they are miserable. If you believe Scripture, then you have to admit Christ never commands anyone to be miserable. Misery is an indicator that you are breaking a biblical boundary.

God's desire is for His children to find joy in their relationship with Him but you will never find joy by choosing sin.

> **Misery is an indicator that you are breaking a biblical boundary.**

You can find joy in your relationship with your horse, but you must shift your view of training. If you do not have the desire or skill necessary to train a horse, then you should purchase a horse that is already trained. When a horse understands and obeys your cues, riding will be pleasurable. This is mutual respect. However, when a horse resists your cues, riding will be frustrating. This is also true in the body of Christ. It is joyful to spend time with saints who have been walking with God and are submitted to Him. But you will probably find less joy in those who resist and cause trouble in the body. Obedience leads to joy in the body. Christ is responsible for training, and you are responsible for obeying Him. When you obey, you will have joy regardless of other people's behavior.

> Training in the body never stops, because there is always a deeper place to go in relationship to Jesus.

If you are not trained up in Christ, then you will not know how to train others. Training in the body never stops, because there is always a deeper place to go in relationship to Jesus.

THE CHURCH'S POSTURE: PRINCIPLE #2
Learn to respect the church by surrendering to the boundary lines that God has set in His Word.

RESPECT THE HORSE: RIDING PRINCIPLE #5
Learn to respect the horse because it was created by God.

Chapter 5: Surrendering Your Way

Chapter 6: Joy in the Body

RIDING PRINCIPLE #6

ENJOY THE HORSE

Riders can find joy in the simple activity of horseback riding. Nothing compares to a strong connection with your horse when you and your horse move together in sync.

Up to this point you have been learning riding principles. While principles are important, they do not represent relationship. When the principles connect to your relationship with your horse, you truly begin to enjoy your horse. Knowing principles does not mean that you know your horse. You must learn and develop a relationship by spending time with your horse. Some people ride horses by feel. For example, they can feel when their horse is on the right lead when cantering. Other people who do not have a relationship with the animal are not as in tune with feeling the horse's movements but rather are heavy on technique and principles of riding.

Technique and principles only serve to keep you grounded and safe in the saddle, but this does not necessarily mean that your body movements and the horse's body movements are in sync. Consider for a moment that you and your horse are so connected that when your body makes a slight adjustment the horse responds. It feels as though the horse is an extension of your body. There is nothing quite like that connection. It requires trust and obedience from both rider and horse. There is a difference between a horse that is learning and a horse that is resisting. There is no joy found in rebellion and resistance. The balance between technique and relationship leads to great joy with your horse. There will be challenges and areas to grow, but you will be able to enjoy the relationship through the process. When your horse is submitted then you will experience true connection and joy.

> Knowing principles does not mean that you know your horse.

> Technique and principles are important but they do not develop the relationship, rather they keep you grounded and safe in the saddle.

Riding on High Hills

Chapter 6
Joy in the Body

"... Then you shall delight yourself in the LORD;..."
Isaiah 58:14

True biblical joy is found in the presence of Jesus and is fulfilled when the body of Christ shares God's desires. God was leading the Israelites in Isaiah 58:13 to understand this principle. In verse fourteen, He shared a benefit of obeying His command for the Israelites to turn their foot from the Sabbath and to stop doing their pleasure on His holy day by calling the Sabbath a delight, the Holy day of the Lord honorable, and honoring Him by not doing their own ways, nor finding their own pleasures, or speaking their own words.

The boundaries God gave to the Israelites would have led them to delight in Him if they obeyed Him. You cannot delight in someone who you do not listen to or agree with. There is a lack of delight in the Lord in our churches today because many are following fleshly desires instead of God's desires.

> Delighting in the Lord comes only by obeying what He says.

If you have not met the requirements God gave in Isaiah 58, then you cannot delight in the Lord because you are still delighting in the flesh. If you walk in the newness of life (Spirit), then you will delight in the Lord and find fullness of joy in and with those who are walking in the Spirit. However, there is sorrow to the Spirit when anyone in the body walks in their old nature. The body will not lose Christ's joy because of some people's disobedience, but the body's joy will not be full. Consider a church where every member is walking in the Spirit of God. What a joy that would be!

Unfulfilled Joy

Scripture reveals that joy is a fruit of the Spirit of Christ. This means that joy is found in your relationship with Jesus not in your relationship with other people. However, your joy can be fulfilled when other people in the church are turning to Jesus, walking with Him, and being likeminded. There are other times when your joy will not be fulfilled. Joy can always be found in your relationship with Jesus, but you won't have external joy in relationships with people living in sin.

> When people in the body fall away from God, there is sorrow.

When people in the body fall away from God, there is sorrow. If you personally fall away from God, your joy will not be fulfilled, and you will extinguish joy in the body.

In order to find joy in the new man, believers must put away non-Christian ways. Ephesians 4:17-19 discusses putting off the old man, and Ephesians 4:20-24 discusses putting on the new man.

> *This I say, therefore, and testify in the Lord, that you should no longer walk as the rest of the Gentiles walk, in the futility of their mind, having their understanding darkened, being alienated from the life of God, because of the ignorance that is in them, because of the blindness of their heart; who, being past feeling, have given themselves over to lewdness, to work all uncleanness with greediness.*
>
> **Ephesians 4:17-19**

Kerry taught:

> *If you recall in Ephesians 4:15-16, Paul wrote in regard to how the church is to work together as a body. We are to function together in unity, and every part of the body has to do its share, because if it doesn't do its share, then it will not function properly. Because of this truth, Paul said, "I therefore testify in the Lord that you should no longer walk as the rest of the Gentiles walk." Paul called for a complete break*

Chapter 6: Joy in the Body

from non-Christian ways. Keep in mind that Paul is writing to believers in Ephesus.

The truth is that this letter is to all believers. Many times you may read the Scripture and think that is not for you because he is talking about non-Christian ways. However, it is important to understand that Paul wrote to believers to make a total break from their old ways since they knew the God who redeemed them. If you are a believer, then this includes you. The Gentiles were a group of people that, according to the Jews, could not have a relationship with God.

The Bible teaches that anyone who surrenders to Christ can have a relationship with God. The Jews believed the Gentiles were totally separated from God. This thinking led them into ungodly ways. Therefore, Paul taught them not to associate with the Gentile mentality or the ways of the Gentiles. Have you ever noticed that spending too much time with non-believers can lead to their ways rubbing off on you? It doesn't take long to get out of shape spiritually.

> **The Bible teaches that anyone who surrenders to Christ can have a relationship with God.**

If you want to get out of shape spiritually, you don't have to do anything. You can just stop reading your Bible, stop praying, stop your fellowship with other believers, stop sharing your faith, stop doing the things you know you need to do, and you will get out of shape spiritually. Paul said, "Stop your non-Christian ways." Then, he moved on to the futility of their minds. Futility here means emptiness or a mind that is without purpose. There is emptiness without purpose. Emptiness is a mind that worships idols. In other words, a mind that worships creation instead of the Creator. That is futile. This type of thinking amounts to nothing spiritually.

Paul taught them that they must make a total break from this kind of living and thinking. You can't have empty, purposeless thinking and be on target as a believer. In verse 18, he stated: "having their understanding darkened, being alienated from the life of God." This is a spiritual death. They chose to be excluded either by ignorance or by the hardening of their hearts. Paul said that you need to stop your non-Christian ways by getting rid of futile thinking and a life that excludes God.

If you are not careful in your own life as a believer, you will serve the Lord with most of your heart and mind, but there will be this one little area you are unwilling to surrender. You may have said something like this before, "I thought I was totally surrendered to God, but through this experience I believe today that I am totally surrendered to Him."

The principle is that you can be totally surrendered to God today and choose not to be totally surrendered to Him tomorrow.

> The principle is that you can be totally surrendered to God today and choose not to be totally surrendered to Him tomorrow.

All people can be ignorant about things in life. What Paul means in these verses is that they are excluded either by ignorance or by the hardening of their hearts. There are three different states of mind to consider.

1. **Innocent Ignorance**: *this is exclusion from the life of God because of lack of exposure to God. It is ignorance, but it is innocent.*
2. **Willful Ignorance**: *this is when a person willfully rejects an idea that has been presented. They have heard about Jesus, but they willfully choose not to follow Him.*
3. **Hardness of Heart**: *this is a numbness. This produces a lack of feeling. This is a state of mind when you arrive at a point where your conscience no longer bothers you. You become hardened, or, as Paul said here, past feeling.*

When you exclude God from your life, you risk a hardness of heart which produces insensitivity. This is a part of being past feeling. Verse 19 states, "Who being past feeling have given themselves over." Pay attention here to the way Paul expressed what brought them into lewdness. He didn't say it took them over without their consent. Rather, he said, "Who being past feeling have given themselves over to lewdness, to work all uncleanness with greediness." When your heart is hardened and you are past feeling, you will give yourself over to sin. In Ephesus and in the Roman Empire, these three issues were huge problems that affected the Gentiles. Paul warned the Christians that they must make a complete break from their old ways.

Sensuality or sexual lewdness was a result of the Gentile lifestyle. They thought sexual immorality, adultery, or fornication was not even a violation. The Roman Empire during this time was evil and lewd. If you study history, you'll see that even in their writing. Their minds were corrupted so that they didn't think on good things, they just did whatever they were thinking. The moment you turn your back on Jesus you are subject to everything. One of the greatest failures of believers in our day is that we think we are smart enough to not fall into sexual sin. This thinking is very dangerous. When you think you have arrived, you are at your greatest point of danger.

> When your heart is hardened and you are past feeling, you will give yourself over to sin.

Why focus on stopping your non-Christian ways when this chapter is about joy? If you desire to experience joy in the body, you must recognize that continuing to live in sin produces sorrow to those who love Jesus and those who love you. When you are deep in sin, you don't always realize that your choices affect the entire body. There are boundaries regarding joy and delight. To delight in God requires following His commands and refraining from engaging in your old way of life.

What God spoke to the Israelites in Isaiah 58 was a conditional statement, just as what Paul spoke to the church at Ephesus was conditional. Many believe the Old Testament is not valid in our day, but it is clear God's Desire is the same in the Old Testament as in the New Testament. To delight in the Lord, you will not be able to live a dis-

> If the church desires that their joy be fulfilled, then the people will have to learn to walk in the Spirit of Christ.

obedient life. There is no joy found in the old way of life for a believer. If the church desires that their joy be fulfilled, then the people will have to learn to walk in the Spirit of Christ. Would you rather bring suffering or joy to the body?

Fulfilled Joy

> *But you have not so learned Christ, if indeed you have heard Him and have been taught by Him, as the truth is in Jesus: that you put off, concerning your former conduct, the old man which grows corrupt according to the deceitful lusts, and be renewed in the spirit of your mind, and that you put on the new man which was created according to God, in true righteousness and holiness.*
> **Ephesians 4:20-24**

Kerry continued in his teaching on Ephesians,

> *According to Paul's writing, there are some things that the redeemed (transformed) need to put away.*
>
> *You will not learn about Christ through non-Christian ways. The only way to learn about Christ is through a relationship with Him by the Holy Spirit. You do not become transformed by following pagan ways and will never be transformed and changed if you continue in those ways. You cannot be radically transformed without encountering Jesus, and you will not remain in Christ without walking in His Spirit.*
>
> *When you were born again, you were born of the Spirit. Now the Holy Spirit guides you into all truth. When you receive the Holy Spirit, you receive all of His comfort, peace, guidance, and joy. All of the fruit of Christ's Spirit dwells in you. You are responsible to apply what Christ reveals.*
>
> *Many believers today know Christian terminology of what it means to be a Christian, but don't know how to live it out. Many of them have never had someone disciple them one on one to help them know how to take the truth of the Word of God and apply it to their life in order to know what it means to "walk in the Spirit so they won't fulfill the desires of the flesh" (Galatians 5:16). Consequently, many Christians are simply confused. They are trying to live the*

Christian life in their own strength based on the principles of Scripture without knowing the Person of the Scripture. The Holy Spirit gives you everything by God the Father through Jesus Christ. All the knowledge you need to know is found in your relationship with Jesus, but you have to apply the truth that you learn from Him.

You can read information about how things are constructed, and know things about that construction, but you may not ever be able to construct anything because you don't have the personal experience to do it. Head knowledge alone is not enough.

> **Head knowledge alone is not enough.**

Paul wrote to the Ephesians about what they need to go beyond their knowledge about Christ and learn to live in Christ. This is true for every believer. When you learn to live in Christ, He gives you wisdom, knowledge, and understanding about practical everyday Christianity. This is more than knowing about who He is, it is pursuing a daily, abiding relationship with Him and living out what He reveals to you.

In order to accomplish this you must lay aside the old self. Before you were born again, your sinful nature dominated your life. Paul wrote in verse 22. "That you are to put off concerning your former conduct the old man which grows corrupt according to the deceitful lust." In other words, you are to lay aside the old self.

The reason many Christians never put off the old and put on the new is they want the new over the old. They don't want to get rid of their old ways and thinking. They just want the new to cover up the old. You are either walking in the Spirit or walking in the flesh, but you cannot do both at the same time.

When Alison was burned in a house fire many years ago, she got a deep burn on her wrist and on her shoulder that needed skin grafts. When she went to the hospital the burns were really dirty. The first thing the hospital did was clean out the burns. This is a painful process but necessary for the wound to heal. If they did not clean the dirty wound but just placed the new skin over the dirty wound, this would cause great infection, and the wound would not heal. This is what many Christians do in their relationships with Jesus. They desire healing, not cleansing because cleansing is painful. Laying truth over a dirty heart will not produce joy. Rather, it will produce confusion and misery. God's truth will not be effective unless you apply it.

> They desire healing, not cleansing because cleansing is painful.

When you have an angry, bitter, unforgiving heart, you must allow God to cleanse that out of you. You must put off your old ways. This means daily abiding in Him through His Word and His Spirit and taking the truth from your time with Him and living it out every day. This is renewing your mind.

Kerry continued,

> *You do not renew your mind by focusing on all your old non-Christian ways but by focusing on God's Word. As you get into His Word, God reveals His Will. Then, the Will of God renews your mind to do the work of God. You will never walk in newness of life apart from the Word of God. It is spiritually impossible for you to be in the Presence of God and remain unchanged. The Word of God renews you and regenerates your thinking. Through reading God's Word and praying, you will constantly adjust from your old nature to your new nature. Prayer is adjusting your life to God. As you spend time in the Word, you will know what to pray.*

The Israelites had to put off their ways in order to delight in the Lord. God told them exactly what they needed to put off in order to put on His Ways. It was up to them to follow through. Many short-change the Old Testament because Jesus had not yet been resurrected. However, the people of the Old Testament did have the Presence of God with them and were able to form a relationship with Him. They just needed to obey Him.

It is important to understand the two sides of the sinful nature, because most focus on behavioral sin. It is important to consider the side

Chapter 6: Joy in the Body

of the flesh that presents itself as clean and polished. There is a side that behaves like a Christian but still has the desire to make a name for itself. These are people who do not struggle with physical addiction, adultery, or murder but still have wicked desires. This type of flesh nailed Jesus to the cross. It is what God dealt with in Isaiah 58. On the outside, they looked obedient but on the inside they loved their own ways more than God. Walking in the flesh, regardless of whether it looks good, will never produce a heart of joy.

For the church to surrender to the way of the Lord, it must submit to the leadership of the Holy Spirit. Considering that the Spirit directed Paul to write so many letters to the different churches, it would seem that as long as we are on this side of heaven, there will always be people who are working against the Spirit. The church needs strong leaders who are willing to stand up for the desires of the Lord and respond properly to those who are striving to thwart the work of God within the church. This is only accomplished when leaders have a deep, abiding relationship with Jesus. When leaders do not correct those who are in opposition to God's Way, they hinder joy within the body.

> **Walking in the flesh, regardless of whether it looks good, will never produce a heart of joy.**

The key to fulfilled joy is to obey the leadership of the Holy Spirit. Correction is not always the response. The Spirit may also lead you to "shake the dust off your feet and move on" (Acts 13:51). The disciples were pushed out from the region they were in because the Jews raised up persecution against them. The disciples responded to persecution by moving on to the next place. It is interesting what the Scripture states happened after it says they shook the dust off their feet.

> **The church needs strong leaders who are willing to stand up for the desires of the Lord and respond properly to those who are striving to thwart the work of God within the church.**

And the disciples were filled with joy and with the Holy Spirit.
Acts 13:52

This is interesting because joy is a fruit of the Spirit. Here it is singled out and used alongside the Holy Spirit. Although this was a difficult circumstance for the disciples, God filled them with joy and the Spirit because they obeyed Him by moving on to the next place. Joy is extremely important within the body of Christ because "the joy of the Lord is your [our] strength" (Nehemiah 8:10). When the Lord filled the disciples with joy and the Spirit, He strengthened them to continue to spread the message of the gospel. When the church obeys Jesus, He fills it with joy and the Spirit! A strong church must delight in the Lord. This is where strength and endurance is found. If you or your church are not experiencing joy, then you are most likely following your flesh instead of the Holy Spirit.

Joy in Fellowship

> *...that which we have seen and heard we declare to you, that you also may have fellowship with us; and truly our fellowship is with the Father and with His Son Jesus Christ. And these things we write to you that your joy may be full.*
>
> **1 John 1:3-4**

Fellowship is an important aspect of being connected to a church body and is the way in which you delight in the Lord. However, many times Christians only focus on having fellowship with others and do not spend time growing in their fellowship with Jesus. When individual members of the body walk closely with the Lord, everyone is unified in the Spirit.

The key between fellowship with God and people is the Presence of the Holy Spirit. When the Holy Spirit is active in a person's life, that person's relationships reflect his fellowship with God. This does not mean this person will never sin, but that when he does sin, he will handle it with God.

For example, let's say that a Christian who is in fellowship with God is attacked by someone in his church and responds in anger. This person then shares with you what happened and confesses his anger was wrong and he has dealt with it with God. This person is not bashing the person who attacked him or spewing his anger onto you and everyone around him. When you are able to see your own sin in the midst of experiencing

Chapter 6: Joy in the Body

an attack it is only because of a strong fellowship with God. The Spirit convicts your heart and leads you to repentance. In these cases, anger does not last long or become a stronghold. When a person is honest at heart regarding what he is experiencing without attacking others, then you know he has fellowship with Jesus.

But there are times when a Christian is not in fellowship with God. To clarify, this would be someone who is born again. It is clear he has a relationship with Jesus but is now acting as though he does. A person out of fellowship with God will usually not see his anger as sin and will blame the person who attacked him for the way he responds. He will either repress his anger or express it. This person speaks of others through anger and ill will. This is an indicator that he is not in fellowship with God. You cannot be in fellowship with God without walking in the Spirit.

> **When you are able to see your own sin in the midst of experiencing an attack it is only because of a strong fellowship with God.**

> **You cannot be in fellowship with God without walking in the Spirit.**

It is important to understand that only God truly knows people's hearts. Jude focused on those who were not born-again but had come into the church and acted like they had been. They caused division because they did not have the Spirit (see Jude 1:19). But in 1 Corinthians 3:1-3, Paul addressed believers who were still acting worldly, or carnal.

> *And I, brethren, could not speak to you as to spiritual people but as to carnal, as to babes in Christ. I fed you with milk and not with solid food; for until now you were not able to receive it, and even now you are still not able; for you are still carnal. For where there are envy, strife, and divisions among you, are you not carnal and behaving like mere men?*
> **1 Corinthians 3:1-3**

In these verses, Paul stated that where there were divisions there was carnality. This indicates that when you live a worldly life, thinking like mere men, you can cause division in the church because you are not walking in the Spirit. There will be a lack of fulfilled joy in fellowship with other believers when there is division, deception, or disobedience within the body of Christ. When you love Jesus with all of your heart, you will love His Church and those in the body. But this is with God's Love not human love. It is not simply acting like a loving person. It means laying down your life for the well-being of the church. You cannot hate the church and love Jesus. That does not go together. Having fellowship with other believers is crucial to having joy within the body of Christ. But getting along is not the same as being unified in Spirit. When you do not walk in the Spirit, you open the door to division and arguing within the body of Christ. But when you allow the Spirit to have access to your heart and other members do that as well, everyone has joy in spending time together.

> *But you, beloved, remember the words which were spoken before by the apostles of our Lord Jesus Christ: how they told you that there would be mockers in the last time who would walk according to their own ungodly lusts.*
> **Jude 1:17-18**

As believers, we join in fellowship with the apostles through Jesus Christ, and they share with us what the Spirit has shared with them. We must remember and keep their words so that we will not be led astray from delighting in the Lord. They told us that there would be mockers in the last times who would walk according to their own ungodly lusts. Why then are we shocked when it happens? It may be that we are not familiar with the Bible or that we are not thinking on it.

> *...for prophecy never came by the will of man, but holy men of God spoke as they were moved by the Holy Spirit.*
> **2 Peter 1:21**

If you are going to delight in the Lord, you must submit to honoring His Holy Day by not doing your pleasures or going your own way. The only way to accomplish this is by walking in the Spirit. Every Word in the Bible is Spirit-led. Therefore, to have joy and delight, in God, believers must saturate their lives with the truth of God's Word and adjust their lives to line up with what they learn. Then, they will experience what it means to ride on high hills.

Riding on High Hills

Riding on High Hills Devotion Chapter 6

Joy in the Body

"... Then you shall delight yourself in the LORD;..."
Isaiah 58:14

The same concept in horseback riding applies to your relationship with Jesus. To truly experience delight in the Lord, you must have a connection with Him through relationship and fellowship. When Jesus was in the world, He had such a connection with the Father that to break that fellowship was the worst pain that He ever experienced. The goal for a Christian is to learn to build that kind of fellowship with Jesus through the Holy Spirit.

It is true that principles and commandments will keep you safe from the danger of sin, but they will never change the desires of your heart. True delight in Christ comes from a complete heart change. When the principles and commandments line up with what your heart desires, you experience true delight. Your heart has to submit to the Word of the Lord and surrender its way in order to experience a deep fellowship with Jesus and find joy.

> **True delight in Christ comes from a complete heart change.**

Establishing Fellowship with the Lord
1. Become consistent in feeding on God's Word. You cannot accomplish deep fellowship by being sporadic in your time in the Word.
2. You must consistently think on God's Word as you go through your day.
3. Learn to seek Scripture to find out what God says about what you face in your life.

4. Pray without ceasing by approaching every decision with prayer.
5. Surround yourself with godly people who are in fellowship with Christ.
6. Meditate on God's Word long enough until you have it deep in your heart to share with others.
7. Continually allow God to examine your own heart and learn to repent of known sin daily.

When you begin this process you will recognize that you are more connected to Jesus and have more joy.

The Church's Posture: Principle #6
True biblical joy comes from the presence of the Lord. To experience this joy your heart needs to have fellowship with Jesus. When you establish this fellowship, you will delight in the Lord.

Enjoy The Horse: Riding Principle #6
Technique and principles are important, but they do not develop the relationship between horse and rider. Rather, they keep the rider grounded and safe in the saddle. Finding joy in your relationship with your horse requires submission through trust and obedience.

Chapter 6: Joy in the Body

Riding on High Hills

Section Three:

The Lord's Blessing

Riding on High Hills

Chapter 7: Honor from God

RIDING PRINCIPLE #7

TRUST THROUGH RELATIONSHIP

Trust goes a long way in any relationship, even your relationship with your horse. Horses are instinctually prey animals. While your connection to your horse is important, your stability as a rider is also important. In the event that your horse's instinct kicks in, you need to be prepared to handle challenges. This helps to keep you safe.

At this stage you should have a strong riding ability and should be secure in the saddle. Any discipline you choose as a horseback rider will be more enjoyable if you and your horse trust each other. If your horse is not a good fit for you or there is no trust in the relationship, then you may not have enjoyable rides. On the other hand when the connection is strong and you are in sync, you will enjoy your time riding .

Think about being on the back of a horse while on a mountain with narrow spaces that have steep cliffs with long drops. This is not a time that you would want your horse to stop listening to your cues. I, Alison, remember an incredible time when my friends and I took a horseback riding trip to France. There were parts of that ride when the guide would say, "Just let go of the reins, hold on to the mane, and let your horse do the work." Those horses had been on those trails many times and were experienced. We had to trust them to keep us safe. They knew exactly how to get through each obstacle.

There was another time when I was on a local trail ride on a horse that I barely knew. This horse was fairly new to trail rides off of its own property. She was not a fan of other horses being around her that were not a part of her herd and would kick if they came too close to her. At one point we were on a narrow path with a big drop off to the right. I was praying, "Lord, get us through this without her kicking." Then someone yelled for us to stop because he hit a bee hive and bees were stinging his horse. At that point, I wanted out of there. The good news is that everyone, including the horses, stayed calm and made it through. It is not fun to be on the edge of a drop off with a horse that you do not trust. I had to lean on my riding skills to keep the horse away from the ledge. She responded well, and I even think she found comfort and trust in my leadership at that time.

Sometimes you will have to trust the horse, and other times the horse will have to trust you. There are times when the horse has more experience in a situation than you do, and other times when you must rely on your skills for safety. In both of these scenarios I did not have any relationship with the horses. In France, I trusted the horse's experience and the guide's instruction. On the trail ride, I trusted what I had learned throughout my years of horseback riding. In order to stay calm in a challenging situation, you must trust something. But when the relationship is strong with your horse, then trust works both ways and a great partnership develops.

> In order to stay calm in a challenging situation, you must trust something.

Chapter 7
Honor from God

"... And I will cause you to ride on the high hills of the earth..."
Isaiah 58:14

In order to ride on high hills, believers must walk in the ways of those who have gone before them in the faith. They must walk in the ways of God. Many times in Scripture, the Lord was with certain people because they walked in His Ways. God blesses those who obey and submit to His Word. There are requirements for receiving the blessing and for continuing in the blessing.

> *These are sensual persons, who cause divisions, not having the Spirit. But you, beloved, building yourselves up on your most holy faith, praying in the Holy Spirit, keep yourselves in the love of God, looking for the mercy of our Lord Jesus Christ unto eternal life.*
> **Jude 1:19-21**

Pastor Josh preached,

> *There is a clear distinction between the people in verse 19 and the people in verse 20. One group were sensual persons, and the other were beloved or dear friends. The sensual people created divisions and factions because they did not have the Spirit, but those beloved were filled with the Spirit. These people had joy, peace, long-suffering, patience, kindness, goodness, and gentleness that comes only from the Spirit of God. Paul discussed this in Galatians 5:22-26: "But the*

fruit of the Spirit is love, joy, peace, longsuffering, kindness, goodness, faithfulness, gentleness, self-control. Against such there is no law. And those who are Christ's have crucified the flesh with its passions and desires. If we live in the Spirit, let us also walk in the Spirit. Let us not become conceited, provoking one another, envying one another."

When you are discerning the signs of apostasy, remember the Word predicted these people would come. Follower of Christ, do not be shocked and awed by it, but be faithful to the Lord in your steps of obedience to Him. Jude told us how to remain faithful. He said to build yourselves up on your most holy faith, pray in the Holy Spirit, and keep yourselves in the love of God.

God's Way

Build Yourselves Up in the Faith

First, Jude encouraged the beloved to build themselves up on a solid foundation. Paul also had encouraged the Ephesians to be built up but not on just anything. They must build on a solid foundation, Faith. Jude started with contending for the faith and ended with building on faith. He did not mean subjective faith but an objective faith. It is the great doctrines of the Bible. The Truth is the foundation for building your faith.

> They must build on a solid foundation, Faith.

Pastor Josh continued,

The building analogy is all through the New Testament. Paul spoke about the fact that believers are the temple of Christ (see 1 Corinthians 3:16). Peter said that Christ is the chief cornerstone of the foundation (see 1 Peter 2:6). And Jesus said in Matthew 7:24-27 that there were two builders. One built his house on the rock. The rivers would flood, and the storms would come, but it couldn't take down the house. The other builder built his house on the sand, and the rains came, and the floods rose, and the house built on the sand collapsed. Friends, we need to build our lives on the Rock, the Lord Jesus Christ. Our eternal purpose on this planet is to build a foundation on the Lord Jesus Christ.

Jude drives it home that we are to build this foundation "on our most holy faith." How do you build a foundation? A spiritual foundation is built on the Word of God, Jesus Christ (See John 1:14). Peter also addresses this:

> Our eternal purpose on this planet is to build a foundation on the Lord Jesus Christ.

Since you have purified your souls in obeying the truth through the Spirit in sincere love of the brethren, love one another fervently with a pure heart, having been born again, not of corruptible seed but incorruptible, through the word of God which lives and abides forever, because "All flesh is as grass, And all the glory of man as the flower of the grass. The grass withers, And its flower falls away, but the word of the LORD endures forever." Now this is the word which by the gospel was preached to you.
1 Peter 1:22-25

Therefore, laying aside all malice, all deceit, hypocrisy, envy, and all evil speaking, as newborn babes, desire the pure milk of the word, that you may grow thereby, if indeed you have tasted that the Lord is gracious.
1 Peter 2:1-3

Often God's blessings in Scripture include lists of what needs to be put off or laid aside. As you are building yourself up in the faith, you will have to lay aside the sinful flesh. If you are going to ride on high hills, then you cannot have sin in your heart. The things that Peter listed are challenges that are faced in all churches. In fact, one of these, envy, is what nailed Jesus to the cross (see Matthew 27:18). These things will not build up your faith, but will tear it down.

Webster's Dictionary defines those sins:

- **Malice**-enmity of heart; malevolence; ill will; a spirit delighting in harm or misfortune to another; a disposition to injure another; a malignant design of evil.

- **Deceit**-an attempt or disposition to deceive or lead into error; any declaration, artifice, or practice, which misleads another, or causes him to believe what is false; a contrivance to entrap; deception; a wily device; fraud.
- **Hypocrisy**-the act or practice of a hypocrite; a feigning to be what one is not, or to feel what one does not feel; a dissimulation, or a concealment of one's real character, disposition, or motives; especially, the assuming of false appearance of virtue or religion; a simulation of goodness.
- **Envy**-chagrin, mortification, discontent, or uneasiness at the sight of another's excellence or good fortune, accompanied with some degree of hatred and a desire to possess equal advantages; malicious grudging.
- **Evil speaking**-speaking ill of others.

You will not know if you have these in your heart if you do not know what they mean or do not spend time seeking God's assessment of your heart. When God causes you to ride on high hills, there will be those within the church who may respond to you out of malice, deceit, hypocrisy, envy, or evil speaking. Building up your faith convicts and challenges those who have no desire to grow. It is important to recognize these in yourself and others so that you are not led astray.

Pastor Josh continued,

> "Therefore, rid yourself of all these little termites: malice, all deceit, hypocrisy, envy, and evil speaking. Like newborn infants, desire the pure milk of the Word so that you may grow up into your salvation" (1 Peter 2:2). The Word of God is pure which means that it contains no sin. The Word of God is trustworthy as a foundation to build up your faith. Therefore, desire it like sincere babes desire milk from their mothers. I love what Charles Spurgeon said: "A true Christian would rather go without a meal than without a sermon."

A true believer would sooner miss a meal than lose his daily portion of Christ. Be sure to read the Word faithfully, systematically, respectively, and obediently. That's how you will build yourself up in the faith.

Riding on high hills means that your heart is so in tune with the Lord that when trouble arises He carries you above it. This means your faith needs to be strong enough to endure whatever comes your way. When the Lord causes you to ride on high hills, your heart and mind do not focus on the struggles and pressures of this world, but on the beauty and majesty of Jesus Christ. Consider the perspective you would have if you were on the back of a horse on a high hill. You would be able to see much of your surroundings. God led the Israelites to this perspective. He asked them to put Him in the proper place in their hearts in order for Him to provide and for them to continue in fellowship with Him. When you live in the Word of God and obey Him, your perspective is heavenly instead of worldly. This not only builds your faith but also provides you with insight into the desires of God's Heart. Knowing God's desires helps you know how to pray.

> Be sure to read the Word faithfully, systematically, respectively, and obediently.

> When you live in the Word of God and obey Him, your perspective is heavenly instead of worldly.

Pray in the Holy Spirit

There are different types of prayer: secret, confessional, intercessory, family, and corporate prayer. But there is only one way to pray the will of God, and that is in Christ through the Holy Spirit. The Holy Spirit prays the Word of God, because the Word holds the desires of God. God designed prayer for you to be able to line your heart up with God's Heart and to cast your cares upon Him. You will not ride on high hills without a developing prayer life. For the Israelites to obey God's commands, they had to surrender their own ways. Surrender is accomplished through prayer. It is easier to try to accomplish things on your own than to wait patiently in prayer. In order to understand the concept of prayer you must think on Jesus. When you wait in prayer, you wait on Jesus. You cannot see everything about your circumstances, but Jesus can. When you are waiting you must remember that more hearts are involved in the situation than just your own.

> Surrender is accomplished through prayer...When you wait in prayer, you wait on Jesus.

Praying in the Holy Spirit does not mean that your prayers are perfect, but that you are asking with sincere faith. God will help you correct and complete your prayers to line up with His desires, and the Spirit will intercede for you.

Pastor Josh continued,

> *"That you would read the Word and that you would pray in the Holy Spirit." This is not talking about praying in tongues. Praying in tongues involves a known language. As I am preaching there is someone translating everything into Spanish, a known language, and it's going into our brothers and sisters' ears who understand Spanish. That is what the definition of tongues is according to the Bible. Many associate the Spirit with speaking in tongues. This is not what Jude taught in this passage. Jude taught to keep in step with the Holy Spirit and through obedience one may be filled with the Spirit. Paul wrote in Ephesians 5:18 that believers need to be filled with the Spirit. In order to be filled with the Spirit, believers must surrender their lives to prayer in the Spirit, submitting to the Ways of the Lord. Prayer is one of the most talked about disciplines but the least practiced. Remember that there is a Father in heaven who wants to hear from you.*

> Being filled with the Spirit is absolutely necessary for you to ride on high hills and complete what God has started in your life.

Being filled with the Spirit is absolutely necessary for you to ride on high hills and complete what God has started in your life. When God causes you to ride on high hills, He will carry you through challenges, persecutions, and difficulties as well as the good times in your life. Only the Spirit of

God can accomplish this. Many Christians are afraid of the Holy Spirit because they do not have an understanding of how bankrupt they are without the Spirit. You cannot accomplish anything in the Kingdom of God without the Holy Spirit.

If you want to learn to pray as Jesus did, you must know Him. The way you get to know Jesus is by surrendering to His Spirit and immersing yourself in His Word. The Word reveals Christ to you as you read and contemplate what He is saying. To know how to pray in the Spirit is to know Jesus, because the Holy Spirit is the Spirit of Christ. The Holy Spirit will do nothing apart from the Word of God. You build confidence in your relationship with Jesus as the Spirit guides you with the Word. Anything guiding you away from the Word is not God. Praying the Word of God in the Spirit anchors your heart to Christ. This makes it difficult for anything to move you away from God.

Keep Yourselves in the Love of God

When God honors you, there will be people who hate you. This is a truth that you will have to accept if you want to keep yourself in the love of God. There is no way to ride on high hills and be untouched by gossip, attacks, and jealousy from people within the church who want what God is giving to you but are unwilling to surrender their lives to Him. Every Israelite in Isaiah 58:13-14 had the opportunity to ride on high hills, but they did not all obey. There is no short cut to keeping yourself in the love of God. You will have to obey what He is telling you or His promises will be void in your life. Obeying means staying within God's boundary lines.

> When God honors you, there will be people who hate you.

God honored Stephen in the book of Acts by carrying his mind during a time of stoning (see Acts 7:54-60). Scripture states, "Being full of the Holy Spirit, [Stephen] gazed into heaven and saw the glory of God, and Jesus standing at the right hand of God" (Acts 7:55). Just before this happened, Stephen had recapped the work of the Lord through the Old Testament all the way to the crucifixion of Christ. Stephen was obedient to the call of God on his life. God caused him to ride on high hills during an awful stoning. Riding on high hills means riding above the response of those who are following the evil one. When you are in a dangerous place on the edge of a huge drop off, you must trust your horse. In the same way, you must rely on your relationship to Jesus when you are walking in the will of God. If you do not have a relationship with Jesus, then you are in danger of a great fall. Stephen's relationship with Christ was obvious by the Spirit's leadership every step of the way. Stephen was in the love of God and was able to endure persecution.

> Riding on high hills means riding above the response of those who are following the evil one.

Kerry was teaching on the book of Ephesians 5:15-21. The amazing revelation here is that Pastor Josh continuously references the book of Ephesians in his preaching on the book of Jude. It is important to realize this because it is the leadership of the Holy Spirit who made these connections.

Before Kerry started teaching on Ephesians 5:15-21, he shared:

> *Elaine, I don't know if you knew this, but I received information yesterday from some people in this community that you and I are moving. Did you know that? I received several e-mails and even phone calls. The first untrue statement was that the pastor is moving to a church in Northwest Arkansas. Then, it was that the pastor and Kerry are moving to a church in Northwest Arkansas. Today, someone called and said the pastor turned in his resignation. There is a vast difference between wisdom and gossip. Gossip does not come from heaven. It comes from the pit of hell because it is a lie.*
>
> *The truth is that the pastor's son is going to Northwest Arkansas to John Brown University to work on his masters and to be a fellow in the Soterquist Institute. From that information, we landed on a lie that the pastor is moving to another church. Then today, I discovered that I'm going with him. It is just not true. God has not called us out of this church, and therefore, you are going to have to put up with us until God calls us somewhere else.*

> Gossip does not come from heaven.

> *If you hear this lie tomorrow, please tell whoever says it that they are not listening to the truth. In fact, if you want to know if I'm moving somewhere, come and ask me. If Elaine and I are planning on moving, you will be the first to know. The truth is that we did not want to move when we came here. We left three grand kids, a son, and a daughter-in-law that lived five minutes away from our house. The reason why we moved here is because God sent us here, and that is the only way that we will leave. Elaine and I follow what God directs in our lives. So I hope that the God who you trusted when He called us here will be the same God you trust if He calls us to move to another church. We have served in churches that are so thrilled by the work of the Lord calling us to their church, but then get mad at us when God calls us to another church. This is not wisdom that comes from above.*

In order to keep yourself in the love of God, you must be interested in God's Way above your own way. Some time after this incident, God did call the pastor and Kerry to a church in another state where Kerry and Elaine met Alison and her family. Many people leave a church when God has not called them to, but not everyone does that. Some are faithful to the call that God places on their lives. God had another assignment for Kerry and Elaine. Through this assignment they met Alison. Then through another call they all met Pastor Josh. You will not stay in the love of God if you do not obey Him when He calls you somewhere else. You must go with God to stay in His love.

Jude completed this section of Scripture, "looking for the mercy of our Lord Jesus Christ unto eternal life" (Jude 1:21). Church body, we must wait expectantly for the mercy of our Lord Jesus Christ for eternal life. As things continue to become darker in the world, remember that Christ will return. As a believer, you have eternal life in Christ that starts now. In order to ride on high hills, you must live according to God's Ways. This means living eternal life now by getting to know the Person of Jesus Christ. Eternal life is knowing God (see John 17:3).

> **In order to ride on high hills, you must live according to God's Ways.**

Honor from God

> *If anyone serves Me, let him follow Me; and where I am, there My servant will be also. If anyone serves Me, him My Father will honor.*
>
> **John 12:26**

> *I do not receive honor from men. But I know you, that you do not have the love of God in you. I have come in My Father's name, and you do not receive Me; if another comes in his own name, him you will receive. How can you believe, who receive honor from one another, and do not seek the honor that comes from the only God?*
>
> **John 5:41-44**

The Church will never grow in love if it honors people more than God. If we as a church body want to represent Christ, our Head, then we must serve Him with all of our hearts. It seems that many have either become so self-focused or people-focused that they either serve themselves or other people above God. This is not a new way of living. This was happening in the book of Isaiah and the book of John. This is the condition of a sinful heart. God's people in Isaiah 58:13 were serving themselves by using God's Ways to keep people in bondage for their own power and control. The Pharisees in Jesus' day could not recognize God right in front of them because they loved themselves. There are some in our day who have convinced themselves that pleasing people is serving God. To please people you have to give them what they want, and what they want is not always what God desires. To please people is to avoid conflict. This is not loving the church but only protecting yourself.

> **The Church will never grow in love if it honors people more than God.**

> **To please people is to avoid conflict.**

Make no mistake, when you obey God's commands and honor Him, you will love and serve people. But the focus must be on God and His desires and not on people. We cannot call ourselves God's church while following our own ways. When we submit to the ways of God, we represent Jesus. Church, it is time to search our hearts and allow the Lord to clean up His House. Let's put Him in His proper place and allow Him to do what He wishes with His body.

Riding on High Hills

Chapter 7: Honor from God

Riding on High Hills Devotion Chapter 7

Trust through Relationship

"... And I will cause you to ride on the high hills of the earth..."
Isaiah 58:14

Love and trust are not the same in relationships with people, but they are one in the same in your relationship with the Lord. You can love a person but not trust that person. However, to love the Lord is to trust the Lord. The difference is that the Lord is trustworthy. When you begin to ride on high hills, God honors you by carrying you above worldliness to a place of protection. This happens through complete trust in the Lord.

Your relationship with your horse is similar to your relationship with people in that you can love your horse but there may be times you do not trust your horse because both horses and people can disobey. They are not always trustworthy. Consistency builds trust with your horse. Horses that tend to be "steady eddies" bring comfort because you know what to expect. You can trust these horses when riding on high hills. This is the place you want to be with the Lord, the place of consistency.

Consistency in your relationship with God brings peace to your heart. You will never experience deep trust when you are sporadic in your time with the Lord. You must get to know Him and His Ways in order to recognize what is of Him and what is not of Him. This only happens in a consistent one-on-one time with Him. If you have experienced what it means to ride on high hills, then you have a consistent daily relationship with the Lord. When He asks you to do something, then you do it. There is no way to ride on high hills without

> To love the Lord is to trust the Lord... Consistency in your relationship with God brings peace to your heart

love, trust, and obedience. The horse carries you through difficult trails, and the Spirit carries you through difficult paths in life. Grow in your walk with the Lord so that you can experience what it means to "ride on high hills."

THE LORD'S BLESSING: PRINCIPLE #7
When you trust in the Lord with all of your heart, you can ride on high hills.

THE HORSE AND RIDER'S CONNECTION: RIDING PRINCIPLE #7
You will not build a strong connection with your horse without developing trust.

Chapter 7: Honor from God

Chapter 8: Living in God's Promise

RIDING PRINCIPLE #8

OVERCOMING FEAR THROUGH RELATIONSHIP

Even if you have a knowledge of horses, the right tools and techniques, proper nutrition for your horse, and a lush, secure pasture, your horse can still respond in ways that you do not understand.

I, Alison, travel back and forth from Texas to Georgia and because of that Pastor Josh has been gracious to spend time with my horse Victor. He grooms him, works him in the round pen, and rides him. Recently, Victor moved to a different pasture, and the spring grass began growing. Victor began to act increasingly anxious and fearful. One day Josh called me to let me know that Victor acted strangely. He shared that a few days before Victor was acting great. Then he decided to put the saddle on and work him in the round pen. He was just going to lunge Victor because Victor had been more anxious lately.

Josh put the saddle on. When he tightened the girth, Victor began running that fence and attempting to jump out of the round pen. When he did jump out of the round pen, Victor ran to the arena and attempted to jump that fence, even though there was a huge open area to get inside. Pastor Josh was trying to settle him down by using a calm voice. When Victor made it into the arena, Josh removed the saddle.

Fortunately, Victor did not have any physical injuries, but he was clearly having mental issues. As Pastor Josh and I processed this, neither one of us were able to come up with a reason for Victor's actions. Josh decided to back up even more and began just being with Victor in the pasture to regain trust. I went out to the ranch a few days later and took Victor out of the pasture. I fed him and started to groom him. When I groomed him on the left side, he was petrified and would shake. This behavior was very uncommon for Victor.

No one knows what happened to Victor or why he responded that way. However, we will take care of him. As you learn about living in God's Promises, keep in mind that there are many things you do not know. You may lose your mind at times and struggle with truth. You may get afraid. Refrain from trying to figure out why and simply adjust your spirit to the Spirit of the Lord. When you do He will feed you with the heritage of Jacob. God is able!

Chapter 8
Living in God's Promise

"And feed you with the heritage of Jacob your father."
Isaiah 58:14

As Pastor Josh continued to preach from the book of Jude, he shared:

The doctrine of eternal security is based on these words: "to Him who is able." That is the bottom line to eternal security. Our eternal security is not grounded in our power but in the very power and nature of our God. A believer does nothing to earn salvation. Christ did it all on the cross for you and for me. It is His great work on your behalf. Eternal security is a truly magnificent promise of hope in assurance. His Promise does not end at salvation but will carry you through your life as you walk with Him in relationship. Whatever situation you are in, God is able to deliver you or carry you through.

> The doctrine of eternal security is based on these words: "to Him who is able."

Now to Him Who is Able

Now to Him who is able to keep you from stumbling...
Jude 1:24

God is able to keep you from stumbling. If you honor the Sabbath, then the promises of God will mark your life. This is all accomplished through the power of the Holy Spirit.

Have you ever been afraid to stumble? Many people have a fear of falling back into the same sins and ways that they battled before God set them free. If you battle this fear, then you must ask yourself if you believe that God is able to keep you from stumbling. The Holy Spirit is your guide and is more than capable of keeping you from stumbling. As you grow in Christ, you should recognize growth in the activity of the Holy Spirit in your life. God's greatest promise is the promise of the Spirit of Christ: "That the blessing of Abraham might come upon the Gentiles in Christ Jesus, that we might receive the promise of the Spirit through faith" (Galatians 3:14). It is God, through the Spirit, Who will keep you from stumbling.

> Have you ever been afraid to stumble?

The Lord's Blessing requires a connection with the Lord. While God does bless people who do not know Him, He does not give the same blessings to those out of fellowship with Him as He does to those in fellowship with Him. For example, Potiphar, received blessings because he knew Joseph, but he did not have the same blessings as Joseph (See Genesis 39:1-6). Residual blessings are not the same as personal blessings. The Lord kept Joseph from stumbling when he was falsely accused. But to those who will not receive Jesus, Jesus becomes a stumbling block. "Therefore, to you who believe, He is precious; but to those who are disobedient, the stone which the builders rejected has become the chief cornerstone, and 'A stone of stumbling, and a rock of offense.' They stumble, being disobedient to the word, to which they also were appointed" (1 Peter 2:7-8). God is able to keep you from stumbling, but you must obey His Word. Disobedience causes you to stumble.

> Residual blessings are not the same as personal blessings.

God is also able to do way more than you ask or think,

Now to Him who is able to do exceedingly abundantly above all that we ask or think, according to the power that works in us,
Ephesians 3:20

Chapter 8: Living in God's Promise

How much do you believe God can accomplish? The basic answer for the Christian is that of course God can accomplish anything, but do you believe that He will?

God is the One whom you should direct your attention, prayers, and desires to. If God has promised it, He will do it without any difficulty. Who else in your life can do anything? There are many people who can fulfill some things for you, but there is only One who can do anything.

God can not only do anything, but also can exceed your expectations. If you ask Christ to help you understand a particular Bible passage, then He can give you understanding far beyond your imagination. No matter how many people you ask about the truth of that passage, no matter how many books you read about that passage, or how long you think on that passage, He can show you more than all of those sources of information in just a few moments. If you ask for peace, Christ can give you peace far beyond any counseling, pills, or positive thinking the world may offer. But, if you ask God for love, He will give it to you far above anything another person can offer. No matter what you think is real, true, and deep love, God's Love takes you beyond your thinking and helps you feel and understand a Love that is not even possible from anyone in this world.

God's blessings are according to the power that works in you, the same power that raised Christ from the grave. "And what is the exceeding greatness of His power toward us who believe, according to the working of His mighty power which He worked in Christ when He raised Him from the dead and seated Him at His right hand in the heavenly places" (Ephesians 1:19-20). Can you believe it? The same energy, strength, and might that God used to raised Christ from the dead, the same power that lives within you.

When you were born again, God used this same power. No other power can save you or give you things beyond what you can ask or think. Christ has all power and placed that power in you by His Holy Spirit. "Exceedingly abundantly" means a degree that cannot be expressed. You do not have the intellectual capacity to think about how much power and love God has placed in you. Yet, He is able to give you more than you could ever imagine. You will begin to discover things about God's Love and Power that you could not realize with your human thinking which leads to His Enlightenment.

God can give you more than you desire, pray for, or think, as long as you walk in His Ways and obey Him. When you obey God's Ways, He establishes you according to the gospel of Jesus.

> God can give you more than you desire, pray for, or think, as long as you walk in His Ways and obey Him.

Now to Him who is able to establish you according to my gospel and the preaching of Jesus Christ, according to the revelation of the mystery kept secret since the world began...
Romans 16:25

In order for the church to live in God's Promises, it must allow the Lord to establish it in the gospel of Jesus Christ. While many churches preach the gospel, are they established in the gospel? This includes not only acknowledging that Christ lived, died, and was buried for your sin but also that He rose again and is still alive. Then, it must live in the Spirit of Christ. The hidden mystery is the Spirit of Christ living in the members of the body. "The mystery which has been hidden from ages and from generations, but now has been revealed to His saints. To them God willed to make known what are the riches of the glory of this mystery among the Gentiles: which is Christ in you, the hope of glory. Him we preach, warning every man and teaching every man in all wisdom, that we may present every man perfect in Christ Jesus" (Colossians 1:26-28).

> It is important to note that recognizing sin and learning to walk in the Spirit of Christ, can look as though someone is stumbling, even though they may be growing.

For the church to submit to the Head, Jesus, it must grow up into the Head. This requires conviction, correction, and change within the body. As God establishes individual hearts in the gospel, the church will grow in Christ. However, many times as God is establishing hearts, it looks as though many are falling away. It is important to note that recognizing sin and learning to walk in the Spirit of Christ can look as though someone is stumbling at first.

Chapter 8: Living in God's Promise

Pastor Josh preached,

> *God promises that He will preserve us from committing apostasy, departing, wandering away, and abandoning the faith. Can a Christ follower fall from grace? Not if God is honest, trustworthy, and true. Noah may have fallen many times in the Ark, but he never fell out of the Ark.*

Is it possible that to be established according to the gospel a type of falling is required? Such a falling is not falling from grace, but, falling out of sin. There is much to glean from Pastor Josh's experience with Victor. Even though the circumstances surrounding the encounter were ideal and pleasant, Victor's reaction was completely explosive. Did you know that when God establishes you according to the gospel, He establishes your heart in such a way that you cannot fall from grace?

I, Alison can testify to this concept. Several years ago, my circumstances were going great. I was counseling in a church, my marriage was doing well, and I had two wonderful children. This is the time that God chose to establish me deeper into the mystery of Jesus, deeper into the Spirit of Christ. He started by convicting me of my anger. This became so intense that I started to feel depressed. I called a friend to have lunch and told her what was happening. Neither of us could identify why I felt this way. There were no outside circumstances that would cause me to feel that, but God was exposing my sinful heart. Through this process He set me free. But it felt like falling. It made me feel out of control. But I had to fall away from sin to live in the grace of God. Those who refuse to fall from sin never experience the mystery of God. Circumstance had nothing to do with my heart. It was my relationship with the Lord that was driving this revelation.

> **You have to fall away from sin to live in the grace of God.**

God has a heritage for those who allow Him to establish their hearts in His Way. This heritage dates all the way back to Jacob in the Old Testament. Through this heritage, God's saints experience the promise of His Word and His Spirit. In order for the church to receive this heritage, it must fall away from the world and from sin.

The Heritage of Jacob

From the time God made His covenant with Abraham in the Old Testament until now, He has been faithful to keep His Promises. Many do not realize the power of the gospel in its entirety. People tend to focus on initial salvation and not a life lived in the Spirit of Christ. Believers should not only die with Christ but also live in Him in order to be fed with the heritage of Jacob. The inheritance of a saint is heaven, and this inheritance begins now not at death.

> The inheritance of a saint is heaven, and this inheritance begins now not at death.

In order for the church to be built up into the Head, it must preach and teach the Ways of Christ. The only way to live in the gospel is through biblical repentance. This is the solution that God provided for the problem of sin. When I found myself with an angry heart, I had a choice to go God's Way or my own way. I chose God's Way. Through repentance I fell away from sin.

There is much knowledge to gain regarding the heritage of Jacob. There are physical aspects of believer's heritage such as: land (Exodus 6:8) and children (Psalm 127:3). God's protection (Isaiah 54:17), the fear of the Lord (Psalm 61:5), and the testimonies of the Lord (Psalm 119:111) are also a part of this heritage. All of this is available to a church that walks in the Ways of the Lord. For the church today, this heritage is not based on genealogy, but on belief in the Lord Jesus Christ. Generation after generation must believe to partake of the heritage. To be fed with the heritage of Jacob, individual believers must stick close to the truth and carry it on to the next generation.

God does not break His covenant or hold back His heritage to those who love Him. If He did, He would go against His nature of faithfulness. The One Who feeds you with the heritage of Jacob is able to keep you in His Way. Your walk with God is not based on who you are, but on the glorious nature of the Lord Jesus Christ. Your role is to obey what God has ordained from the beginning of time, and Christ's role is to "keep you from stumbling, and to present you faultless before the presence of His glory with exceeding joy" (Jude 1:24).

Pastor Josh preached,

> *God has made a commitment that He would preserve those who are in Christ. God watches over those who believe and love Jesus, and by His omnipotent power He keeps them from falling into sin. This means that those who are in Christ are preserved in Christ and are under His care. He has promised to protect you from falling away. He also has the ability to present you unblemished in glory. This is the result of God's activity in the lives of His people.*

This is feeding you with the heritage of Jacob. When the church submits to and obeys Jesus, it understands that it is God's activity that brings glory, not the activity of people. It is the Spirit of Christ living in the members of the body that fulfills the promises of God.

> **It is the Spirit of Christ living in the members of the body that fulfills the promises of God.**

The Promises of God

The promises of God are accomplished through the gifts that He has provided the church, His Word and His Spirit. (see Galatians 3:14).

The theme of obedience flows through the entire Bible, because the Promises of God are only found in the Lord Jesus Christ. If you are not in Christ, then you are in sin. There is no alternative. You will never obey God's commands if your motive is to receive promises. Rather, you will obey when your motive is to love the Lord. You will not persevere through hardships if your focus is not on God's Promises. Perseverance comes through loving the Lord Jesus. In order to train the church in love, the Lord has to discipline

> **Perseverance comes through loving the Lord Jesus.**

and correct those who do not love Him. If you are in disobedience to the Lord, then you are loving yourself, not God. This is hard to accept but you must accept it. It is even harder to accept that those you love may not be loving God.

When you disobey God's commands, you are choosing to live in sin. Jesus died to set you free from sin. He was beaten to rescue you from yourself. When you choose to love your sin, you are trampling on the work of the Lord. This is devastating to a church body. When you are part of a church body and you disobey by living in sin, then you are putting the entire body at risk. If God provides His Promises to a disobedient heart, He would not be a loving Father. It is not loving to bless sin because it keeps the body of Christ in darkness and is not a good witness to a watching world.

> When you are part of a church body and you disobey by living in sin, then you are putting the entire body at risk.

However, when a church body chooses to stay close to God's Word and His Spirit, the power of the Spirit provides all God's promises to that church body. When God feeds you with the Heritage of Jacob, He feeds you with blessings from Heaven. A good challenge for you as you continue to grow in Christ is to recognize His Promises when you read His Word and write down the Promises that you recognize in your life and the life of your church.

Here are a few of the Lord's promises:

- **Abundant Life in Christ**

    The thief does not come except to steal, and to kill, and to destroy. I have come that they may have life, and that they may have it more abundantly.

    John 10:10

- **The Crown of Life**

    Blessed is the man who endures temptation; for when he has been approved, he will receive the crown of life which the Lord has promised to those who love Him.

    James 1:12

- **A Heavenly Mansion**

    Let not your heart be troubled; you believe in God, believe also in Me. In My Father's house are many mansions; if it were not so, I would have told you. I go to prepare a place for you. And if I go

Chapter 8: Living in God's Promise

and prepare a place for you, I will come again and receive you to Myself; that where I am, there you may be also. And where I go you know, and the way you know."
John 14:1-4

- ### Cleansing from Sin

    I am the true vine, and My Father is the vinedresser. Every branch in Me that does not bear fruit He takes away; and every branch that bears fruit He prunes, that it may bear more fruit. You are already clean because of the word which I have spoken to you.
    John 15:1-3

- ### Deliverance from Evil

    The Lord will rescue me from every evil attack and will bring me safely to his heavenly kingdom. To him be glory for ever and ever. Amen.
    2 Timothy 4:18

- ### Eternal Life in Christ

    For God so loved the world that he gave his one and only Son, that whoever believes in him shall not perish but have eternal life.
    John 3:16

    And this is eternal life, that they may know You, the only true God, and Jesus Christ whom You have sent.
    John 17:3

- ### Fellowship with Jesus

    that which we have seen and heard we declare to you, that you also may have fellowship with us; and truly our fellowship is with the Father and with His Son Jesus Christ.
    1 John 1:3

- ### Fruitfulness

    Remain in me, and I will remain in you. No branch can bear fruit by itself; it must remain in the vine. Neither can you bear fruit unless you remain in me. "I am the vine; you are the branches. If a man remains in me and I in him, he will bear much fruit; apart from me you can do nothing.
    John 15:4-5

- **God's Protection**

   No weapon formed against you shall prosper, And every tongue which rises against you in judgment you shall condemn. This is the heritage of the servants of the LORD, And their righteousness is from Me," Says the LORD.
   Isaiah 54:17

- **Growth in Christ**

   And He Himself gave some to be apostles, some prophets, some evangelists, and some pastors and teachers, for the equipping of the saints for the work of ministry, for the edifying of the body of Christ, till we all come to the unity of the faith and of the knowledge of the Son of God, to a perfect man, to the measure of the stature of the fullness of Christ, that we should no longer be children, tossed to and fro and carried about with every wind of doctrine, by the trickery of men, in the cunning craftiness of deceitful plotting, but, speaking the truth in love, may grow up in all things into Him who is the head—Christ—
   Ephesians 4:11-15

- **Fullness of Joy**

   As the Father loved Me, I also have loved you; abide in My love. If you keep My commandments, you will abide in My love, just as I have kept My Father's commandments and abide in His love. These things I have spoken to you, that My joy may remain in you, and that your joy may be full.
   John 15:9-11

- **Spiritual Fullness**

   Then Jesus declared, "I am the bread of life. He who comes to me will never go hungry, and he who believes in me will never be thirsty."
   John 6:35

- **Spiritual Strength**

   I can do everything through him who gives me strength.
   Philippians 4:13

- **Spiritual Understanding**

  I gain understanding from your precepts; therefore I hate every wrong path.

  Psalm 119:104

- **Victory in Jesus**

  for everyone born of God overcomes the world. This is the victory that has overcome the world, even our faith.

  1 John 5:4

- **Wisdom from Above**

  If any of you lacks wisdom, he should ask God, who gives generously to all without finding fault, and it will be given to him.

  James 1:5

Praise the One who is able to keep the church from stumbling until the day the Lord returns! You may be looking at your life much like the way Pastor Josh and Alison are looking at Victor's fearful behavior. We had no idea what happened and no idea how to help Victor. But there is a God in heaven Who knows what is going on in your life and knows exactly how to help you in whatever challenges you face. The Lord Jesus loves the church more than any human can ever understand on this side of heaven. Why would the church ever believe that God cannot help with whatever challenges come?

The challenge for your church is to love the Lord your God with all your heart, soul, mind, and strength (see Matthew 22:37). Then the Lord will provide wisdom to equip the body to heal the hurting or lost. Sometimes God uses His creation to teach us spiritual lessons. In this case He used Victor to train us to depend on Him for everything. As long as we think we know what to do, we will not need God. It is when we do not know what to do that we turn to Him in prayer!

> **Why would the church ever believe that God cannot help with whatever challenges come?**

Riding on High Hills

Riding on High Hills Devotion Chapter 8

Living in God's Promise

"And feed you with the heritage of Jacob your father."
Isaiah 58:14

Believers must realize that God's Way provides all of the promises that are found in His Word. However, there may come a time in your life when something inside of you is just not right. You begin to feel unsettled and cannot figure out what is wrong. You may have been walking with the Lord in an honest relationship, but all of a sudden you feel out of control.

What happens when you can't figure it out or when relying on your own way is not working? Regardless of how it feels, this is a great place to find yourself for spiritual growth to happen. Abiding in Christ does not mean that there will never be a time of internal struggle. In fact, when God is ready to grow you, He has to show you areas of your life that need to change. This will not take you out of fellowship with Christ as long as you are honest with Him in prayer. Instead you will grow in dependency and intimacy with Him. It is about perspective. You must stop seeing struggle as a bad thing and begin to see it as an opportunity to grow in your relationship with Jesus.

> Abiding in Christ does not mean that there will never be a time of internal struggle.

The same is true in your relationship with your horse. When there are times of struggle, don't allow it to change the way you view your horse. Instead, see it as a learning opportunity. This is the only way to develop as a horseman. Struggle is important because without it there cannot be growth.

THE LORD'S BLESSING #8

The Lord blesses us with His Spirit to guide us in the timing and delivery of His Truth.

THE HORSE AND RIDER'S CONNECTION: RIDING PRINCIPLE #8

A horse is a prey animal created with instincts that protect them from danger. Regardless of the trust you have built with your horse, they can act out of character at any moment. When this happens, you need a patient spirit to overcome whatever conflict arises. Place your trust in God. He created the horse and you.

Chapter 8: Living in God's Promise

Chapter 9: Confidence in God

RIDING PRINCIPLE #9

CONFIDENCE THROUGH RELATIONSHIP

Love builds confidence. You may be a fearless rider who can get on a horse and jump a four-foot jump, open up the horse in a full gallop, or run barrels at full speed, but what happens when the horse gives you trouble? Do you have enough of a relationship with your horse to have confidence to correct bad behavior?

It will take patience and consistency to bring Victor back to where he was before his incident. I, Alison, went out to the ranch recently to put a saddle on Victor. First, I took him out of the pasture and fed him. While feeding him, I groomed him. I noticed that he was much better than the last time. This was positive. After grooming him, I took my western saddle pad (which is a fairly large saddle pad) and showed it to him. He snorted and backed up. I was not able to get anywhere near him. I then tucked the pad underneath my arm and started leading him. He was much more curious when the pad was moving away from him rather than toward him. Once he relaxed, I tried again. I was able to touch him with the pad, but it was clear that he did not want me to put the pad on his back.

I decided to get my English riding saddle pad (a much thinner, smaller pad) and see how he would respond. He was much calmer with this pad, and I was able to put it on his back. I left it on him and let him eat and walk around with it on his back. I decided that was enough for the day. Putting a saddle on Victor has not been an issue until he experienced something that scared him. If I love him, I will not force anything on him that scares him, rather I will let him choose. This requires throwing away my agenda and taking it slowly. My agenda was to put the saddle on Victor, but I was only able to get the saddle pad on him. I needed to be ok with that and try again next time. Confidence is found in love and consistency. It is critical to understand that forcing him is not love, but control.

> Confidence is found in love and consistency.

Riding on High Hills

Chapter 9
Confidence in God

The mouth of the LORD has spoken.
Isaiah 58:14

The existence of the church needs to begin and end with God. A church that loves Him will obey Him when He speaks and have confidence that He will do what He says He will do. When God led *Think LifeChange* to Flat Creek church, the church responded through the leadership of Pastor Josh. He recognized the work of the Spirit. It was no coincidence that a ministry that Pastor Josh followed from its beginning in Texas visited the church where he was the pastor. The Lord is more than capable of leading His church the way He desires. The church must love God and find confidence in Him alone.

Confidence in God comes when the church is walking in the Spirit and is able to recognize God at work. There are many ways the church can respond in the flesh instead of in the Spirit. Many leaders in churches are building their own kingdoms and not the kingdom of God. When this happens, God's activity will threaten them. Therefore, they will not want to support God's activity and will make the body insecure instead of confident.

The Church's Response to Truth

The body of Christ has a great responsibility to recognize what is of God and what is not of God. Why would we say that *Think Lifechange* was sent by God to Flat Creek or any other church? *Think Lifechange's* main message is Jesus' message of repentance. Any church aiming to build themselves up in the faith, pray in the Holy Spirit, and keep themselves in the love of Christ will not avoid this message. If a church desires to stand until the second coming of the Lord Jesus Christ, it must discern between the people, programs, and events designed to destroy it, and those designed to build it up in Christ. The body needs to pay attention to the teaching of Jesus when making decisions for the church, not who or what they prefer.

> The main message is Jesus' message of repentance. Any church aiming to build themselves up in the faith, pray in the Holy Spirit, and keep themselves in the love of Christ will not avoid this message.

The only way to train the church in love is to train the church in Spirit and in Truth. Angry people can teach truth, but they will have no power. It is critical that the church body recognize that "the heart is deceitful and desperately wicked" (Jeremiah 17:9). This means every heart, not just the apostates that Jude warns us about. This truth should drive the church body to submit to God's Ways and continue learning and growing in the Holy Spirit. If we do not, then we will be in the same situation as those in Jude's day. In fact, many churches are in that situation today.

Jude provides a road map on how to continue your life with God. He stated that we must "build ourselves in the faith, pray in the Holy Spirit, and keep ourselves in the love of God" (Jude 1:20-21). This is the only way to receive what God has for the church and find true spiritual confidence. Many pastors and church leaders may be insecure about their positions. Instead of confronting their insecurity, they often continue walking in the flesh. This causes more insecurity. The church cannot operate with the mind-set of the world and expect to have spiritual confidence. The greatest area of struggle in the church is not salvation but continual spiritual growth. The body must

> The only way to train the church in love is to train the church in Spirit and in Truth. Angry people can teach truth, but they will have no power.

continue to grow spiritually in order to grow in their confidence into the Head.

When leaders and members are stunted in growth, the body suffers and has division. For example, members may get into a leadership position and begin slandering those who discipled them. This may lead to these people leaving the church. The pastor of the new church they attend is warned about their deception but responds, "Well they have not done anything wrong to me." Therefore the new pastor feels free to place them in leadership. However, even if those people did not personally slander the new pastor, they are a danger to the whole body. The person who slanders another saint within the body is a danger to all saints in the body, whether or not they directly slandered the pastor. Falsely accusing a saint is an action against God. If you are a pastor, then you are not training the church in love if you place these kind of people in leadership. Not only may this hurt other people later but this also makes those in the wrong think they were right. Because there is no consequence for their wrong, they will be stunted in spiritual growth. Boundaries and consequences are wonderful training tools. Without them a person will go his own way believing he is following God. This is not love. Love does not avoid conflict but faces and corrects it. This does not mean that you fight with people, but that you remove them from leadership and offer help in the hope that they will receive it.

Confidence doesn't come from knowing God's promise, but from loving God with all your heart, soul, and mind. In order to love God while serving in leadership, you must be willing to lay down your life for the security of the body. If you do not surrender your leadership style to Christ, then you will lead the body in your ways instead of God's Way.

> When leaders and members are stunted in growth, the body suffers and has division.

> Falsely accusing a saint is an action against God.

> Love does not avoid conflict but faces and corrects it.

The only hope for the church to remain in the love of God is a deep fellowship with Christ. Otherwise, the church is open to every false teaching that enters. You can know Scripture, but without Love you will not have confidence.

Love provides a choice. When someone is out of line, he has a choice to continue in his wrong way or submit to God through repentance. What he chooses is his responsibility. There are consequences when people choose to continue the wrong way. It is important that church leaders and church members allow there to be consequences for wrong actions. Because without consequences, there is no need for the person to change. God's love disciplines those who need correction.

> Because without consequences, there is no need for the person to change.

While there are those who grumble, complain, mock God's Way, and continue in their own ungodly lusts, those who flatter people are just as bad yet much more subtle. Everyone loves to have his ego stroked from time to time. However, the church should not allow a person to flatter his way out of consequences.

Is it possible that we confuse love with control? Controlling someone is not love. Self-protection to avoid feelings of insecurity is control. Allowing people to make their own decisions requires confidence. For the church to love someone who is in rebellion or disobedience, it must give that person over to God. Love does not force but allows for choice. Desiring to force people to obey God is control. A church with leaders who are walking in the Spirit will be able to discern a true repentant heart from a person who is only speaking words of repentance. Spiritual confidence only comes when the church and its leadership is walking in God's Ways. This is a true relationship with Jesus.

> Controlling someone is not love.

Spiritual Confidence

> *But recall the former days in which, after you were illuminated, you endured a great struggle with sufferings: partly while you were made a spectacle both by reproaches and tribulations,*

Chapter 9: Confidence in God

and partly while you became companions of those who were so treated; for you had compassion on me in my chains, and joyfully accepted the plundering of your goods, knowing that you have a better and an enduring possession for yourselves in heaven. Therefore do not cast away your confidence, which has great reward. For you have need of endurance, so that after you have done the will of God, you may receive the promise:
Hebrews 10:32-36

The Lord's blessing includes spiritual confidence. This means having confidence in God not in self or anything else. In this passage, the Christians had endured suffering for the sake of Jesus. Maybe your church is in a season of suffering for the sake of Christ. If this is so, Paul's writings are for you just as much as for the Christians in his day. It is important to keep a heavenly perspective. You do not need to have a negative mind-set. You did not make it this far in your walk with God to lose confidence before the journey is complete. What God started, He will complete. If you have lost confidence, then your perspective has shifted off of God and onto something else.

Confidence is trust or faith that a person or thing is capable. The world teaches us to have self-confidence. Over-confidence is having unmerited confidence in someone or something. Being unconfident leads to anxiety and can paralyze a person. Hebrews 10, Isaiah 58, and Jude all teach to place confidence in only One person, the Lord Jesus Christ. When your confidence is in the Lord Jesus you will have courage. The Spirit of Jesus gives you what you need to walk through what God has called you to do.

The more we are around leaders, the more we observe that many say they trust God but their spirits reveal something different. When you have confidence in God, your spirit will be at peace. However, if you have been living your life placing your trust in self or others, you have false thinking that God must break down in order for you to see that He is the only One you should trust. This breaking down is difficult until God opens your eyes to the truth. Any person or thing that you place your

> **When you have confidence in God, your spirit will be at peace.**

confidence in is dangerous to your mind because those things can be taken away. Take a moment and think about what danger the church faces when its leaders are not placing their confidence in God.

When Victor acted out, it was clear that something had hurt or scared him. Whatever it was, he lost confidence and trust in us. When someone or something hurts or scares you, you should not lose confidence in God. Instead, you should lean on God with all of your heart. The church as a whole needs to lean on Jesus, the Head, when it is hurt or scared.

The most amazing time of church growth in church history was during the greatest times of persecution. It seems to be more difficult to have courage during times of peace. We tend to take for granted the benefits and freedom that we have in worship in times of peace. We must never forget that spiritual confidence comes from a deep walk with God through obedience. This means following God's Way no matter what circumstances the church faces.

If persecution came to the church today, many would give up the faith or lose courage. The author of Hebrews warned about such action in verse 35, "Therefore, do not throw away your confidence, which has a great reward." If anyone is following Christ to receive a reward on earth, then they misunderstand the reward. Christ is the great reward. Therefore, we should follow Him with a deep desire to know and love Him, not to simply receive rewards.

> Christ is the great reward.

During times of peace our tendency is to stop spending time with the Lord, praying, or sharing our faith. Why do these things seem to dissipate when things are going well? We seem to view the peaceful times as the great reward. It is during those times that we tend to believe that we have succeeded. This is when the church is in the greatest danger. Our walk with God should never diminish, no matter if it is during times of peace or persecution. Do not forsake your first love. Christ is your greatest reward!

What if we treated the peaceful times as a time of preparation for the next crisis. If we did this, then we would be ready to endure and walk through the crisis with the strength of the Lord. This is why the greatest reward on this side of heaven is Jesus Himself. There is no greater reward. Through abiding in Him continually you can be ready for whatever you will face, even if it is death. As humans, we tend to think that some of the worst things that can happen are persecution, major sicknesses, broken relationships, or major natural disasters. Yet, the worst thing that can happen to the church is to lose its confidence in and fellowship with Jesus.

> Yet, the worst thing that can happen to the church is to lose its confidence in and fellowship with Jesus.

The writer of Hebrews prompted believers to recall how they have suffered and how believers from the past had suffered during times of struggle and persecution. Can you recall what your spirit was like during a time of struggle? A believer should be full of love, joy, and peace during times of persecution. Our confidence in the church needs to lie in the truth that when we come to a place of crisis, as long as we are walking in fellowship with Jesus, He will supply His Spirit and His Truth to comfort us and help us endure. When we are not walking in fellowship with the Lord, we will not be confident in difficult times. Spiritual confidence is not gauged by the number of baptisms, salvations, or members, but by the church's spirit and response during times of difficulties. When the church responds by striving and fighting each other, the church is acting like "mere men." This promotes spiritual insecurity.

Spiritual Insecurity

In Isaiah 58, God addressed His people; and the book of Jude addressed God's people about apostates. The sin of a believer has the same result as the sin of an apostate. Paul calls believers who continuously act like mere men, carnal (see 1 Corinthians 3:3). Therefore, believers must learn how to walk in the Spirit of God, or the church will be spiritually insecure.

When God supplies an answer to a church that has been praying, some will receive the answer and some will not. Those who cannot receive God's answer are those who desire their own will and their own way. To discern whether or not something is from God, one must spend time in His Word, prayer, repentance, and obedience. If the church is not approaching Jesus for guidance in how to lead, then they are merely going their own way and acting like "mere men."

Flattering words are not a substitute for a heart surrendered to Jesus. This means that you cannot automatically assume that someone is walking in fellowship with God by word alone. A person's response during times of conflict and difficulty is a clearer indication of that person's walk with God. This is why Jude was adamant about going beyond salvation. We must stop people who are walking in the flesh from leading the church. Spiritual leadership requires spiritual people. Some may sneak into a position based on flattering words, but Love needs to step in and make a correction if it becomes evident they are not walking with God. God's Love is for the entire church body. If one individual is harming the whole body, then God's Love will remove that person for the protection of everyone involved. There are no favorites in God's eyes. He loves both those who love Him and those who do not love Him.

> Spiritual leadership requires spiritual people.

Victor has always been easily afraid, but he has confidence in certain areas. Much of his fearfulness stems from not being exposed to different things. He has not been off the property often and does not have a significant amount of riding miles on him. One major reason for this is because his job is mainly to be used in equine biblical counseling. Since having an experience that scared him so badly, it will take some time and patience to bring him back to where he was before that experience. The church body is no different. Every church has strengths and weaknesses. Every church experiences circumstances that may leave them scared. It may take time and patience to bring certain members to where they need to be spiritually. But the key to confidence is trusting in Jesus Christ, the Head. Did you know that Jesus is coming back? When He does, how would you like Him to find your church? Do you want Him to find your church acting like "mere men" or acting like people who love Him with all their hearts? If the church is to be trained up in love, it has to follow the Lord Jesus Christ. Focus on Jesus and learn what it means to ride on high hills. The result is spiritual confidence.

Chapter 9: Confidence in God

Jesus is Coming Back

Now I saw heaven opened, and behold, a white horse. And He who sat on him was called Faithful and True, and in righteousness He judges and makes war. His eyes were like a flame of fire, and on His head were many crowns. He had a name written that no one knew except Himself. He was clothed with a robe dipped in blood, and His name is called The Word of God. And the armies in heaven, clothed in fine linen, white and clean, followed Him on white horses. Now out of His mouth goes a sharp sword, that with it He should strike the nations. And He Himself will rule them with a rod of iron. He Himself treads the winepress of the fierceness and wrath of Almighty God. And He has on His robe and on His thigh a name written:

KING OF KINGS AND LORD OF LORDS.
Revelation 19:11-16

How well do you know Jesus? Jesus walked the earth in gentleness and meekness as an example of how believers are to walk with God. Though Jesus is the perfect Lamb of God, it is critical that we all understand that He is coming back to judge in righteousness. It is critical that the church focus on growing in the love and understanding of the Savior, Jesus Christ. We must abide in Him until His coming. If the church wants to be trained up in love, it must set all of its attention on Jesus. He is the only Way.

And now, little children, abide in Him, that when He appears, we may have confidence and not be ashamed before Him at His coming.

1 John 2:28

Pastor Josh concluded his sermon series on Jude:

"Jude brought this short but powerful letter to a close with a doxology, a word of praise to our only God and Savior through Jesus Christ, our Lord. A doxology is a response to the saving work of God and is a recognition that it is all God's work. He receives all the credit, glory, and the honor. This doxology calms our fears and fuels our hopes. This doxology brings joy to our theology. It is the outshining of His character in nature.

Praise God for His saving work, for His powerful radiance, for His greatness, for His complete and moral security and splendor. Everything about God is glorious. "The Son being the brightness of His glory and the express image of His person, and upholding all things by the word of His power, when He had by Himself purged our sins, sat down at the right hand of the Majesty on high," (Hebrews 1:3). When we praise God, we praise the most magnificent Person in all of the universe. He is not simply King, but He is King of Kings. He is not simply Lord, but He is Lord of Lords. That is Who we worship. We praise Him for His power, and His authority. He is glorious and majestic. He has dominion and power. His glory, majesty, and power will keep us.

To God our Savior, Who alone is wise, Be glory and majesty, Dominion and power, Both now and forever. Amen.
Jude 1:25

The Lord's Blessing is Jesus!

Jesus alone is our confidence.

Chapter 9: Confidence in God

Riding on High Hills Devotion Chapter 9

Confidence in God

The mouth of the LORD has spoken.
Isaiah 58:14

Victor is a horse that never had a problem putting the saddle pad or saddle on until something happened that scared him. Now the saddle pad represents something terrible to him.

Consider that the saddle pad represents God's Truth. God is approaching His church and speaking His Truth, but how is the church responding? Is the church responding out of fear like Victor or out of disobedience, desiring to go its own way? Perhaps the church is responding

out of obedience and applying the Truth that God is speaking. Just like Victor is stalled in training until we can put the saddle pad back on him, the church is stalled in growing spiritually until it realizes that God's Truth must be central to its existence if it wants to follow the Head of the church, Jesus Christ.

Now consider that we were able to get the saddle pad on Victor. The truth is that we still need to get the saddle and the rider on in order to claim that he has overcome his fear and that he is a fit horse to ride. The church cannot only preach and hear Truth, but it must also surrender and walk in the Ways of God through His Spirit. In Isaiah 58:14, God told the Israelites exactly what to do in order to ride on high hills. They had to surrender and obey His Words. When Scripture states that "the mouth of the Lord has spoken," it means that this is the only Way. Either the church will walk through trials God's Way or they walk in disobedience.

> **The church cannot only preach and hear Truth, it must surrender and walk in the Ways of God through His Spirit.**

THE LORD'S BLESSING #9

The Lord provides every Word, direction, and guidance to His church. The church must walk in His Will with a heart of Love.

THE HORSE AND RIDER'S CONNECTION: RIDING PRINCIPLE #9

If you love your horse, then your connection is much more than fun. Love produces a desire to continue even when it is hard. Love will be your confidence as you continue to learn and grow in training.

As of the date of this publication, we are excited to share that we were able to put the saddle on Victor!

Chapter 9: Confidence in God

Riding on High Hills

Other Books Available at www.thinklifechange.com

My Spirit is Life and Peace!
Alison Veazey and Kerry L. Skinner

What truth do you base your life upon? What if you found out that what you have based your life upon is not truth? Do you believe that the Bible is absolute truth? Until you invite the Holy Spirit into your heart by accepting Jesus Christ into your life and believe that God's Word is absolute truth, you will not live in the peace that God has for you. The Holy Spirit is the only One Who can teach you the truth found in God's Word. Christ died to leave us with His Spirit. His Spirit is Life and Peace.

Philippians: From Anxiety to Peace (workbook)
Alison Veazey and Kerry L. Skinner

A seven week Bible study on the book of Philippians.

Many focus on joy when reading the book of Philippians. However, at the time we started to write on the book of Philippians, our ministry was flooded with those struggling with anxiety. Pastors invited us to speak to groups about dealing with anxiety. Individuals came for counseling to deal with their personal anxiety and lack of peace. God made it clear that the focus of this study should be peace and contentment that frees a person from anxiety, tension, worry, and stress. One thing that is clear in Philippians is that the Spirit of God does not give you anxiety. Anxiety manifests as a result of focusing on yourself. When you depend on yourself, you will be anxious. When you love and depend on your Shepherd, Jesus Christ, you will receive peace.

James: Walking in God's Love (workbook)
Alison Veazey and Kerry L. Skinner

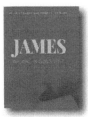

A seven week Bible study on the book of James.

God's Love is a theme that runs through the entirety of the Bible. The book of James is no exception. Some have called it the Proverbs of the New Testament. Many Bible studies written on the book of James focus on faith. However, in processing the book of James, we found that none of the truths are possible without God's Love. It would seem that many read the Scripture for knowledge about God, without considering the Love of God. This produces a lack of depth in relationship to God and others. There is a depth of God's Love that Christians have not even tapped into yet. A Love that is unexplainable. This is the reason that this study is focused on love. As you begin this study, commit to allowing God to reveal your heart. God loves you, but do you love Him?

John: True Belief Brings Joy (workbook)
Alison Veazey and Kerry L. Skinner

A seven week Bible study on the book of John (part 1 of 3).

By inspiration of the Holy Spirit, John wrote this gospel account to help us keep on believing. John writes of the beginning being the WORD, Jesus. The rest of the book is about the difference Christ can make with those who are sinful, need a relationship with the Savior, and choose to believe. There is nothing you will ever face that He does not know about. He provides everything needed to live in this world. Jesus came to love and teach you to depend on Him for everything that you need in your life, for without Him you can do nothing. This study will guide you into a deeper and more personal relationship with Jesus.

Gifts from God (365 day devotional/journal)
Alison Veazey and Kerry L. Skinner

Gifts from God is a 392 page devotional/journal beautifully bound and in a classy imitation leather cover. A place is provided on each page for writing your own journal notes. The perfect gift that goes on and on. This devotional depicts the authors' personal walks with God, one day at a time, for 365 days. The goal is to help God's people learn how to sit in His counsel and allow His Word to change the spirit of the reader to be more like Christ. This alone will reveal God's power to our fallen world.

My Word is Like a Fire!
Alison Veazey and Kerry L. Skinner

Is there a difference between simply reading the Bible as a book and reading it because you have a relationship with Christ? After sharing and talking with thousands of people and after years of learning to walk with God, the authors have come to understand that many people do not know the difference. This book is written from the truth of the Word and from many life experiences to help believers move beyond simple Bible reading to an intimate relationship with Jesus. We pray God will use this book to bring you face to face with the Word of God–Jesus!

The Joy of Repentance
Kerry L. Skinner

In many ways, the Body of Christ has forsaken the biblical mandate to repent, defining the process as negative and burdensome. But in reality, sin produces a yoke of bondage and consequence, while repentance provides a roadway of reconciliation. The suffering Christian, soiled with the residue of this world, is only a repentant prayer away from resolution and healing.
The Joy of Repentance reveals that:
• Confession of sin is common. Repentance of sin is rare.
• Though sin truly is negative, repentance is positive

The Heart of the Problem Workbook
Henry Brandt, Kerry L. Skinner

An interactive, Scripture-based workbook that shows readers how to fight sin effectively and live a more problem-free life. This helpful workbook gives encouragement to everyone who has ever faced an insurmountable situation. Pride, anger, and denial separate people from the solutions and comfort they long for. By seeking God's answer, even the most complex problems can be solved once and for all.

The Word for the Wise
Henry Brandt, Kerry L. Skinner

Worldly solutions offer people only temporary relief from their problems, but biblical counseling offers a trustworthy and lasting cure. This book shows ministers and other counselors how to help angry, broken, confused people look at their lives from a biblical perspective, and move beyond the situation of the moment to the real underlying cause of pain and disappointment. *The Word for the Wise* contains a wealth of real-life examples, along with guidelines for the qualifications, attitude, methods, and standards of professionalism for biblical counselors.

The Christian Life: A Human Impossibility
Kerry L. Skinner

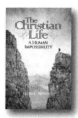
Learning the basics of Christianity is relatively simple–if knowledge of the how-to's are all that interest you. Simply listing the commands of Christ does not require a massive amount of time nor an in-depth study. Putting into practice the commands of Christ is quite different! This book helps you understand in a practical way what it means to walk in the Spirit.

Breaking Free From the Bondage of Sin
Henry Brandt, Kerry L. Skinner

A human approach to dealing with sin does indeed relieve symptoms. But there is no human remedy for the problem of sin. The cure is out of this world. Only God can help. This book will help to illuminate the barriers [sins] that come between a person and the resources available from God through Jesus Christ. Jesus came to save us from our sins. If there is no human remedy for sin, should we not pause and take a careful look at the biblical definition of sin and its cure?

Marriage God's Way
Henry Brandt, Kerry L. Skinner

Tragic but true, couples who follow the world's models of marriage end up in divorce. This problem is growing more and more prevalent even in the church. But *Marriage God's Way* takes a fresh and frank new look at how to ease marital strife by considering marriage from a biblical perspective. With personal illustrations and applications, this book reveals God's plan for marriage and how we must approach this sacred relationship with a higher Christian standard of love. Only God can join two people in wedlock, and only God can keep their love for each other alive.

I Want to Enjoy My Children (11 week workbook)
Henry Brandt, Kerry L. Skinner

If you didn't plan for them–or even if you did–having kids may threaten to spoil the fun of marriage. This book shows how to make parenting a fascinating, pleasant journey, wherever it may lead. This biblical, practical guide is based on the truth that parents need help from a resource outside themselves–God. With anecdotes, examples, and meaningful Bible references the authors show how to develop an inner peace with God to navigate the twists and turns of family life–and make it enjoyable!

What's In Your Backpack? (Kid's Version)
Hannah (Mergist) Lederman

Teaches the *Steps of Repentance* on a kid's level. Based on *The Heart of the Problem.*
What's in Your Backpack? (Kid's Version) is a companion journal to the Leader's Guide with worksheets for each lesson and journal pages for each week.

What's In Your Backpack? (Leader's Version)
Hannah (Mergist) Lederman

What's in Your Backpack? (Leader's Guide) has 7 lesson plans going through the 5 steps of repentance for children, including object lessons, review and discussion questions, and memory verses.

Do You Have Your Walking Shoes On? (Kid's Version)
Hannah (Mergist) Lederman

Put On Your Walking Shoes (Kid's Version) is a companion journal to the Leader's Guide with worksheets for each lesson including space for a personal quiet time and journal pages for each week..

Do You Have Your Walking Shoes On? (Kid's Version)
Hannah (Mergist) Lederman

Put On Your Walking Shoes (Leader's Guide) has 7 lesson plans going through 5 steps of walking in the Spirit for children, including object lessons, review and discussion questions, and memory verses. lessons, review and discussion questions, and memory verses.

Wings as Eagles
Hannah (Mergist) Lederman

Wings as Eagles dives into what it means to wait on God according to Isaiah 40:31 and encourages busy people to slow down and listen to God's Word. Spirit for children, including object lessons, review and discussion questions, and memory